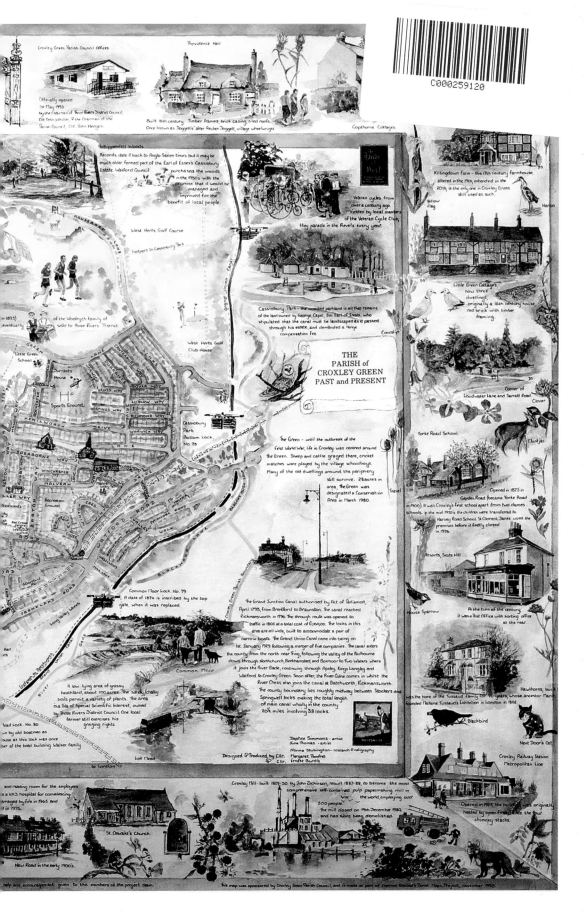

"Out & About in Croxley Green"

With

John Pilgrim

Written by John Pilgrim

Photography by David Thrower

Edited by Margaret Ward and John Pilgrim

Printed and Published in 2007
By Alpine Press

Alpine Press Limited
Station Road
Kings Langley
Hertfordshire
WD4 8LF
Tel: 01923 269777

ISBN 978-0-9528631-8-2

TABLE OF CONTENTS

In the Beginning . . . .

Durrants House 3

Richard II, Wat Tyler and the Peasants' Revolt 9

Meanwhile Back In My Childhood 10

Rousebarn Lane 1

So is it Rowcebarn, Rosebarn or Rousebarn? 12

West Herts Golf Club and Pilgrim's Golf Club 1

West Herts Golf Club 1

More Childhood Memories and More History as Well 10

Redheath, Simmonds Nursery and York House School 17

John Dickinson - The Canal and the Mill 2

John Dickinson 24

The Dickinson Paper Making Process 2

The Canal 28

Cassiobury Park 30

Cassiobury 32

To the Woods! 30

Walk One - Whippendell Woods 37

Walk Two - Woodland Trust Woods 39

Walk Three - Quiet Lanes 4

Walk Four - The Grand Union to Croxley Green 4

Walk Five - Cassiobury Park Heritage Walk 4

Scots Hill 40

Scotbridge Mill 48

Education in the Broadest Sense 50

Windmills on my Mind 52

The Good Old Village Green 5

Some Places on the Green 53

The Revels 57

Croxley House 60

Copthorne Road - 'Chess Side' and Number 73 6

Number 73 Copthorne Road 60

The Mystery Baroness 67

Some of the Pubs (More Later) 68

Some Ways a Young Lad Could Make Some Extra Cash 7

Croxley Great Barn 70

The Annual Garden Competition 78

"Metroland" 80

The Places of Worship 8

The Boys' Brigade 87

The Railway Stations 90

TABLE OF CONTENTS

New Road 93

The Guild House' 94

Barton Way? Well Maybe 95

Marie Tussaud and Croxley Green 96

The Schools 97

Durrants School 98

Brother George 99

Sister June Remembers 100

Little Green Lane School 101

Malvern Way School 104

Yorke Mead JMI 105

An Says 107

Croxley Common Moor 108

The River Gade 109

Some Croxley Pleasures and Pastimes 111

Croxley Wanderers 112

Croxley Camera Club 113

Croxley Green Gardening Club 116

The Croxley Green Conservation Area Committee 117

Croxley Green Wine Guild 118

Croxley Green Library 120

Croxley Green Old Time Dancing Club 121

Royal British Legion Croxley Green 122

Memories of Milson Watkins 123

Keep Croxley 'Green' Group 124

The Croxley Green Mummers - A Christmas Tradition 125

The Jazz Workshop 126

Richmond Way - A Personal Indulgence 127

The Colonel 128

Ice Cream Sundays 129

Did He or Didn't He? 130

Bungee Jumping in Croxley 132

Croxley Park 133

More Croxley People 134

Basil Martin Wright 135

The War Memorial 137

The Prefabs 138

Finally - And in No Particular Order 140

A Walk Down Memory Lane 143

Bibliography 149

The North End Boys 152

ACKNOWLEDGEMENTS

A book such as this requires the help and assistance of many people if it is to get off the ground and David Thrower and I were greeted with enthusiasm and a smile everywhere we went in Croxley. Listed below are the names of individuals and groups who supplied historical information, photographs, advice and memories for our project. I might have missed some because there were so many, but rest assured that our visits to Croxley were always something to look forward to and that your contributions were gratefully received. We would like to say a special thanks to Croxley Parish Council's Chairman Mark Saxon, Clerk to the Council David Allison and all members of the Parish Council, Croxley Camera Club, Croxley Gardening Club, St Oswald's Church, St Bede's Church, Methodist Church, Fuller Way Church, the Baptist Church, Rob Rees and Lee Tyson and the Hertfordshire Countryside Management Team.

THANKS TO:

Margaret Ward for editing and research, Bill Pilgrim, George Pilgrim, June O'Mahoney, Linda Seeley, Sue Scott, Jan and Eric Field, the head teachers of Rickmansworth School, Harvey Road School, Yorke Mead School, Malvern Way School, York House School, members of various clubs, societies and organisations in Croxley Green for their contributions, assistance and the photographs they supplied, Milson Watkins, Stella Davis, David Harding.

Throughout the book we have used some photographs David Thrower took of the beautiful work carried out by Croxley Needlecrafters Stitch Club while they were in the process of producing their Croxley Quilt. I am most grateful to them for allowing us to use the pictures and found their work quite stunning so thanks to: Stella Davis, Sue Burch, Gill Thomson, Gill Cooksey, Anne Wynne-Jones, Barbara Pope, Vivien Tunwell, Adelheid Jenkins, Cheryl Day, Pam Miles, Sheila Botten, Clare Fox, Alison Crookes, Lynda Porter, Elaine Norman, Maygan Marsh, Liz Lindley, Audrey Sims, Mary Vaughan and Vanessa Munroe. Artist John Kirkham allowed the group to use some of his artwork in the construction of the quilt.

Croxley Green has always had a special place in my heart. I was born there and have wonderful memories of a childhood that would be the envy of many a modern child. I have nothing against computers (this book was written on one, for goodness sake!) and I have nothing against other modern technology, but I often wonder if too much time spent in front of various screens instead of getting out and about is a useful way to grow up and gain experience. I often hear older people slating off the younger generation and muttering "What do they know?" and, to a certain extent, I agree with them because I was able to gain experience through being around older people who didn't appear to be in a hurry. Modern Croxley is a bustling place compared to the village I knew as a child but it retains a great deal of its charm and the community seems to have a real sense of place, which is good. It would be unwise for children to wander through the woods or along the canal towpath for hours on end as we did. Nor would a walk into nearby Watford through Cassiobury Park at night to go to the cinema be advisable. In the summer school holidays our parents hardly saw us from dawn until dusk because we would be off building camps on West Herts Golf Course (and being chased by the greenkeeper) or being Robin Hood in Whippendell Woods, when Valerie Smith was allowed to be Maid Marion.

This book includes some of the history of Croxley Green but it is not a history book in the true sense. I wanted to make a record of the village, a place that I remember fondly as somewhere that 'real people' live and work. Along with photographer David Thrower I spent a year retracing my childhood and meeting the people who live in Croxley now. It was an enjoyable experience for both of us; for me the benefits are obvious but for David it was the chance to photograph a really photogenic place and to take his time doing it.

John Pilgrim, Sandy, Bedfordshire 2007.

It always snowed in winter when I was a kid because we had proper seasons of the year back then! If it wasn't snowing on the day I came into the world then I like to think that it was and there isn't anyone to disagree with me. I was born on December the sixth 1942, at the end of another hard year for a war torn world, the end of a year that Winston Churchill summed up thus: "It is not the end. It is not even the beginning of the end. But perhaps it is the end of the beginning." I like to think that 'Winnie' might have been alluding to the fact that another little Pilgrim might make a difference but, in truth I still don't really understand what he was talking about and, anyway, I had more important things on my mind.

Just to prove my point about snow in winter here is a shot of
All Saints' church dressed for the occasion!

I was the fourth child born to Ivy Dorothy Pilgrim (formerly Stanton) and Arthur George Pilgrim and the first to be born in Croxley Green. By the time I came howling into the world my sister June was busy helping Mum to control my two brothers, Bill and George. The family had moved from London to the countryside where it was considered safer and where my dad had a reserve job. My brothers had decided very early in the piece, that school was a place not to visit if it could possibly be avoided and so they spent a great deal of time observing aerial 'dog fights' between the Royal Air Force and the Luftwaffe. This avoidance of the academic life must have been passed down the male Pilgrim line because, a few years later, I took much the same route. There again, perhaps it was quite simply a new life in the countryside that was the attraction. Farmyards were places where tractors operated and animals lived, orchards were places where fruit grew and waited for grubby little boys to 'scrump' it before it was completely ripe.

'Punch', the family dog, was born in London and blotted his copybook on arrival in Hertfordshire by stealing the Sunday joint from Auntie Nellie's kitchen table! She wasn't really our auntie any more than her husband Herbert was our uncle but Mum, Dad, Bill and George all squeezed into their cottage at the top of Little Green Lane and they were joined later by June who was, for a short time, evacuated to Dorset.

Nellie and Herbert's Cottage is to the left in the above picture. The pond is still a haven for wildlife although there's far less water in it these days!

George was the youngest Pilgrim when the family left London and there was (and in fact still is) a ten year gap between him and me so I remember nothing of the war years. My earliest memories include going to school in a Scout hut, going to school in St Oswald's church and then going to a brand new place of education at Malvern Way before moving on to Little Green Lane Junior Mixed where Mr Worthy ruled with a rod of iron. It was whilst I was spending a day avoiding Mr Worthy and his staff that I had a conversation with Auntie Nellie that was to fire my interest in history.

At around 8.50 am one spring morning I decided to bypass Little Green Lane Junior Mixed and continued on up the lane until I reached the village pond opposite Nellie and Herbert's cottage. I spent a pleasant half an hour swinging out across the pond from a willow tree, thinking about looking for frog-spawn and getting a shoe full of water before Nellie spied me from her kitchen window. She was much too smart a lady to enquire as to why I wasn't at school and, instead, she told me the history behind the row of cottages where she lived. It wasn't much of a history to be truthful, but Nellie told it in such a way that I was hooked and wanted to know more. Crafty old girl, that Nellie!

So what follows is a history of Croxley by way of my own small tribute to a nice lady and with grateful thanks to those people who have taken the time to seek out and chronicle the pre-Pilgrim years at Croxley.

View of Croxley House from Baldwins Lane

In 1016 'Croc' was the royal administrator for the area now known as Croxley Green. As part of his job he assessed the value of the Green for King Canute. The name 'Crocs Leah' (Leah meaning a clearing) was adopted and later became Crockeslegrene and finally Croxley Green. Those are believed to be the bald facts but my Auntie Nellie told it differently. She said that Croc was employed by William the Conqueror and some 20 years later 'Crocs Lea' appeared in that august document, the Domesday Book and that is how the place got its name! So it's off to the great book itself to try to clear up this small matter before we move on. So what did I find? Well, in a way both explanations are right. Croc was indeed a 'moneyer' to King Canute and he did report the existence of property in the area in 1016 but his name also appears in the Domesday Book so I think we can accept that our village takes its name from the old boy.

In Croc's time whoever lived in the area would have gleaned an existence from the wild game in the woods and the materials for clothing and building would have been garnered from the woods as well. Tracks would probably have appeared over the years across the green and through the woods. Life would have been pretty Spartan. Nearby Rickmansworth provided a living for some fifteen families so we can guess that Croxley was even smaller.

Richard de Croxley goes down in history as the first person to have his name placed on record as an inhabitant. He was a knight in 1166 and gave a mill in Croxley to the Nunnery of St. Mary at Clerkenwell. In the year 1248 a farm is recorded as having been owned by Ralph Pyrot and another in 1278 as being owned by Simon Duraunt. You may find these two surnames familiar and you would be right because they still exist today in roads, estate and street names. Anyone live in Parrots or Durrants Drive, or indeed, attend Durrants School?

Durrants was known to us kids as Old Merchant Taylor's and indeed it is now the headquarters of the O.M.T. Society, which has well over three thousand members worldwide. The O.M.T. Society is made up of former pupils of the Old Merchant Taylors' School. Durrants is also a country club with sporting facilities including rugby, cricket, hockey, squash and snooker. It became Durrants Club Limited in 1977 but the history of the area where the house stands goes way back to 1278. When it was farmed by Simon Duraunt it was part of a Manor of Croxley which Offa, the Saxon King of Mercia, gave to St Alban's Abbey in AD 790.

In AD 757 to 796, Before Croc, Offa, a fearsome and warlike man was the Saxon King of Mercia. He gave his daughter in marriage to Ethelbert, King of East Anglia and promptly did away with the groom during the marriage ceremony! He then took over Ethelbert's kingdom and added it to his own. Later Offa converted to Christianity and finally founded a monastery at St. Albans as well as showing remorse for what he had done by making many endowments to St. Albans, among them one of the four manors of Rickmansworth which later became Croxley. It didn't do the old boy any good because he died shortly afterwards and presumably was as despised in death as he had been in life. In 1326 when Abbot Richard de Wallingford of St Albans returned from Rome after the Pope confirmed his election, he stayed at the Manor House in Croxley; he was a leper and a man noted for his scientific knowledge. In 1539 the Manor became Crown property when Henry VIII dissolved the Abbey and it was leased to William Baldwin. Elizabeth I sold the Manor to Dr. John Caius, who founded Gonville and Caius College at Cambridge in 1557 and endowed the Manor on the college. When William Baldwin's lease on the Manor House expired the rights were transferred to Dr. John Caius by Elizabeth I. He was a well educated man who had served the queen as a physician. He also gave his name to one of the 'houses' at Rickmansworth Grammar School which I attended sporadically!

Around 1860 Thomas Woods became the tenant; he was a partner in the famous auctioneering establishment now known as Christie's. He bought some land from the College and commissioned what was described by The Times as "a red brick, stone and tiled moderate sized mansion". Woods' initials are above the front door. When Woods died in 1906 his collection of paintings and drawings was valued at half a million pounds, not bad for a chap who only lived in a moderate sized mansion! Durrants was sold to Charles Morland Agnew and Sons who were fine art dealers, and when he died in 1931 the house was sold to the Watford building company Headstone Estates. It was this company which developed much of the surrounding estate with semi-detached housing. Merchant Taylors' purchased twenty five acres from Headstone in 1936 and developed the land as a sports ground, the mansion becoming the club house. During the Second World War the house was requisitioned by the council and it was returned to O.M.T. in 1949.

I am indebted to J.W. Birch (Hon. Librarian and Archivist to the O.M.T. Society) for the above information.

Durrants House Main Entrance

These trees surround the area where the ornamental pond used to be.

Many different sports have been played at Durrants over the years, above is the cricket umpires' entrance

The Clock Tower at Durrants

The author on the main staircase at Durrants

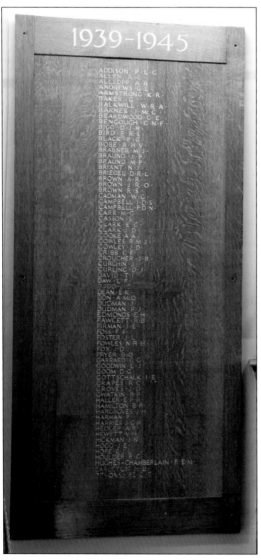

In 1349 the Black Death struck down over half the kingdom and peasants who had purchased their freedom were pressed into becoming serfs again, as a result of the lack of labour. Some years later a certain Red Dickon the Elder was arrested for the murder of Roger of Bachenworth. He was found guilty and his son, unsurprisingly named Red Dickon the Younger, was sentenced as an outlaw. The boy took to the woods around Croxley. Red Dickon and his band became linked with Wat Tyler and the Peasants' Revolt.

Richard II, Wat Tyler and the Peasants' Revolt

Richard II came to the throne in 1377 aged 10 and John of Gaunt became Steward of England. John of Gaunt was unpopular with the businessmen of the City of London, the clergy and the commoners of Parliament. He wanted to re-establish the authority of the Crown and the Royal Family. He had at the end of Edward III's reign removed the Chancellor and the Treasurer and replaced them with his own men. 'The Good Parliament' spent the rest of Edward III's reign trying to overthrow Gaunt's men and at the start of Richard II's reign politics were complicated and unsettled.

The country was over-taxed and when in 1381 an extra poll-tax was introduced, the peasants of Kent and Essex rebelled. They gathered behind Wat Tyler and marched to London. The Chancellor and the Treasurer were beheaded by the mob on Tower Hill. The young King met the mob at Smithfield where Wat Tyler presented their charter. Tyler attacked the Lord Mayor of London as he tried to arrest him and he was later beheaded. The London revolt was effectively over. Meanwhile, in St Albans the local townsmen drained the Abbot's fishpond, killed his game, sacked the houses of his officials and burned the charters that gave him his manorial rights. There is a story about the men of Croxley banding together with those of Rickmansworth and Cassio and marching on St. Albans Abbey. Red Dickon finally proved his father's innocence and Oswald of Croxley was exposed as the real murderer.

The area around Norwich Way was a wonderland when I was growing up. The land, which had once been part of the Durrants estate, hadn't been developed then and the old ornamental pond was home to magnificent newts and other wild life. There were also huge fir trees and other cultivated plants growing amongst the wild flowers. The land was simply perfect for camp building (that's building a camp rather than being camp whilst building) and useful if a small boy decided to run away from home! One summer's day Peter Prigger and I were playing in a wigwam we had made out of an old blanket in my back garden. We got to arguing about something and when I petulantly threw the old meat skewer we were using as a tent peg into the ground, it bounced up and caught Peter on the cheek. He made an awful fuss and my mum appeared with only one thing in mind, a clip around the ear for me, so I ran. I didn't stop running until I was safely in the woods where I sat on an old anthill and took stock. I decided that I would do a Robin Hood and live in the woods. I was certain that my family would come looking for me and resolved to disappear into the trees when they did.

Busily I collected some old bits of corrugated roofing that had been dumped and used them as the roof for my new home (a hollow in the ground). I collected as many 'vinegar leaves' as I could, I was convinced that one could survive by eating a plentiful amount of the leaves and some of the sour fruit from surrounding trees. There were some flaws in my plan and they soon became obvious. To start with, the 'vinegar leaves' would have been best left growing in order that they would be fresh when I ate them; next, the roof of my hovel was clearly going

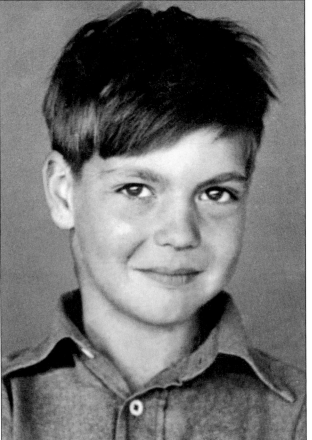

to leak when it rained and finally, none of my family appeared to be searching for me. I couldn't understand where they were, after all I had been away from home for at least half an hour. Why weren't they rushing towards me right now with tears in their eyes and asking for forgiveness? After another half an hour I decided to slope off home (it was tea time). I slunk into the kitchen where my mum ignored me and I went upstairs considering suicide because then they would really miss me. As it turned out there was a 'Merry Miller' cake for tea so I decided to give the rest of the family the benefit of my company.

The author as an angelic little boy, my how times change!

The lane was the place where Mum and Dad took us for a walk on Sundays. It was a good stroll from Rousebarn Farm, which stood on the corner of Little Green Lane and Rousebarn Lane, to the Clarendon Arms at Chandlers Cross but it was worth it.

Once we had negotiated the first part of the walk with Whippendell Woods on our right (the wood was a good place to run on ahead of the parents and arrange two or three ambushes as per Robin Hood or Billy the Kid), we would stop off at 'The Log Cabin' for a cup of tea or lemonade and maybe a piece of cake. The cabin is still there and I visited Ralph Hitchcock whose family have lived on the site since he was a small boy. It would have been Ralph's grandma who served us our treats on Sunday afternoons. Part of the log cabin remains as does Blacketts Nurseries where Ralph was brought up much in the style of 'The Good Life'.

Ralph's grandparents William and Katharine moved from London where William worked at County Hall to Bushey then into Whiteshack Farm (later renamed 'Freeholme' and remains today standing close to the M25 at Chandlers Cross). The purchase of the land at Blacketts came in 1953, where the family got down to keeping various animals and growing their own produce. Ralph well remembers wandering happily through Whippendell Woods as a lad and still enjoys the solitary life at Blacketts, which grew into a successful and well regarded nursery under the stewardship of his father Bill. It must have been a tough life but a healthy one!

Ralph and JP

Ralph's Bedroom

Ralph's Storeroom

Ralph's House

So is it Rowcebarn, Rosebarn or Rousebarn?

Well, all three really. Henry Rowce probably gave his name to the lane as he is mentioned as being in the area in 1527. In 1766 the lane is recorded but shown as Rowsbarn and some ten years later as Rosebarn.

This barn was, I think, once owned by a farmer named Sansom. When I was a child we used to play in and around the barn. When I returned to Croxley I was rather sad to see it in such a state but things were about to get worse.

Just a few days after David Thrower had taken his photograph of the barn on the previous page, a violent storm totally destroyed it.

Riders making their way along the lane towards Whippendell Woods.

West Herts Golf Club and Pilgrim's Golf Club!

Close to where Cassiobridge House used to stand is a small field where, as kids, we mad our own makeshift golf course. We chose the field for two reasons: one, it slope considerably which tested our golfing skills and two, it was as close as we could get to Wes Herts Golf Course without trespassing! As I recall we only had three or four clubs to shar between us and we got our supply of tees and balls from West Herts - not the shop, but from the course. We would hide in the ferns halfway down the first fairway and wait for a player to make an errant stroke into the bushes before dashing out to claim our prize. Tees were a little more difficult because we had to wait until a player left the teeing off area before rummaging around in the bin that was there to receive discarded tees.

West Herts is a beautiful course bounded on one side by the Grand Union Canal as it passe through Cassiobury Park and on the other by Rousebarn Lane. The woods which surround the course were a popular area to play in and, when I walked through them again (at th tender age of sixty three), I remembered rolling down a steep hill into a bed of tall stinging nettles, being attacked by wasps, shot at by 'Fatty' Davis with his airgun, chased by irate golfers and having a quick kiss and a cuddle with a girl named Anne. It is sad to relate tha kids no longer enjoy such simple pleasures these days and the once well worn paths through the woods are mostly gone. There used to be a large hollow tree in the middle of the gol course and it was a bit risky crossing the fairway to get there but it was worth it because there were some wooden steps inside and a small boy could ascend to dizzy heights and observe golfers trying to hit balls out of the rough. We learned a lot of useful words from those players!

This was our golf course, the first tee was in the bottom left-hand corner of the field and all of the holes were a par three but for Dudley Withers par six or seven.

West Herts started life at Bushey Hall in March 1890 when thirteen enthusiasts formed the club. In 1896 the club received permission from the agent of Lord Essex to play golf over his land at Cassiobury and work began on the new course in June 1897. The course was designed by 'Old Tom Morris' who was born in St Andrews, Scotland. He was a true pioneer and exponent of golf, an accomplished champion, course designer and club-maker. Morris lived in a time when golf was the preserve of the affluent due to the cost of handcrafted wooden clubs and 'featherie' balls. Growing up in St Andrews, he would have been surrounded by golf and indeed his first job was apprentice ball maker to Allan Robertson. Old Tom Morris died in the year 1908 aged 86, as a result of sustaining a fractured skull after falling down the stairs in the New Club, St Andrews. A classic example of not keeping your eye on the ball and your head still, Tom!

The statue was donated to the golf club by life members. The sign is for the benefit of the public!

We have already seen some evidence as to how various places in Croxley came to be named and yet another is about to be revealed. From around 1539 the manor was held by William Baldwin for forty four years. The name of Baldwins Lane (a place where I spent many happy hours courting various local lovelies) is said to have come about through Margaret Baldwin. Her name is in the parish registers for 1581, more about her family later.

In 1545 the name William Jacket shows up and the Jackets were a well known family locally until the 17th century. So when Peter Priggen, Dudley Withers, 'Fatty' Davis and I were sledging down Jacotts Hill in winter time from West Herts Golf Course into Rousebarn Lane, we were travelling a well worn route!

Redheath holds yet another special place in my heart because the Simmonds family of Chipperfield had one of their plant nurseries there. My first job when I left school was as a trainee salesman for Burton's the Tailors in Watford but I left after a few months to do a stint at Simmonds where Pete Dormer was in charge of shrubs and plants and a certain 'Mac' McComish (I think that is how his name was spelled) cared for the roses. 'Mac' was a real hard taskmaster who enjoyed a drink or three and we youngsters often suffered a tongue lashing by way of helping him to relieve his hangover. Phil Simmonds, the youngest of the Simmonds boys, taught me to drive the old, grey 'Fergie' tractor and allowed me to take the wheel of his wartime Willis Jeep as well, so that was how I learned to drive!

Simmonds Nurseries in the 1960's. Left to right, Phil Simmonds, Pete Dormer, the Author and Big 'Mac'

'THE BIG HOUSE'

We called it the big house at Redheath and indeed it was and is large and is now a very fine school known as York House. The main house has quite a past. I am indebted to the headmaster of the school for allowing me to refer to the history of the house as written by a former head, Patrick B. Moore.

Redheath is not mentioned in the Domesday Book but it is a fair bet that, since Rickmansworth was quite a large settlement, the local peasants managed some sort of an existence in the area. In his book Patrick B. Moore tells us that when snow melts in the park it reveals evidence of ridging and ditching, which is a good sign of previous farming. The Baldwin or Baldyn family settled in the area in the 15th century and remained for at least two hundred years. The 1525 baptism register for the parish of Watford shows the birth of Henry Baldwin of Redheath. We also know that, between 1659 and 1666, another Henry Baldwin purchased land in the Sarratt area and that the estate stood at around 500 acres. Thomas, son of Henry, died in 1709 and his nephew Charles Finch inherited the estate.

York House School.

In 1712 Charles Finch built the present house. The last of the Tudor building was demolished in the 1950s but the stables and barns still remain as converted residential dwellings. It is said that Finch employed Sir Christopher Wren to design the building and the dates certainly fit. Charles Finch passed away in 1718 and ownership of the house passed to Henry Baldwin Finch. In 1725 mourners were sent a rather unusual invitation to his funeral. In his book Patrick B. Moore describes the invitation thus: It showed a recumbent figure about to be buried and surrounded with lighted candles and banners and was liberally decorated with death's heads, crossed bones and a funeral procession complete with undertaker, two mutes, mourning relatives and servants, and said *"You are desired to accompany the corpse of Henry Finch*

Esquire, from his late dwelling house at Redheath to the parish church at Watford on Sunday 28th of this instant November at twelve o'clock precisely. And bring this card with you". The Finches planted a number of trees in the park and the rotted stumps of some of them can still be seen in the woods.

Scrumping time at York House!

Old clock in school reception.

Old photograph of the way things used to be at York House.

In 1888 Reverend George Finch is recorded as the owner of the house and at the end of that century ownership passed to another Henry Baldwin Finch. Soon after this the Finches let the house and the new tenants, the Peto family only stayed a short time. The Newall family took over the house and the sculpture of the soldiers in Watford near the Town Hall is known as the "Newall Brothers Monument". As far as I understand it the story goes like this: The three Newall boys fought in the First World War. The youngest brother, Nigel, died in 1917. The eldest brother, Leslie died in France in 1915. A letter was discovered in 2001 which was written to Nigel's mother by a fellow officer in the Army. The letter, dated October 14, 1917, explained the circumstances of Nigel's death.

I cannot tell you how dreadfully sorry I am to have to tell you that Nigel was killed instantaneously on Friday morning at 5 minutes past 6. All my officers had been wounded, and he was sent to me to help me as I was in a rather bad unpleasant place with no officers. The Germans were being heavily shelled and he and I were watching from our shell hole to see if the Germans were going to retire, and we would have shot them and followed them, and as Nigel got up to shoot at some of the enemy he was hit by a bullet in the middle of his forehead.

I cannot tell you how dreadfully sorry I am for you. He was such a splendid person and was simply worshipped by his men and loved by all of us, he will be most terribly missed.

It was a great blow to both of us that he did not come to my company, but all the same we managed to see a lot of each other. I think he looked on me as his best friend, as we were the only men of the old lot left out here. It is terribly sad, I cannot get over it. We were so pleased to be together those few hours, and he behaved so well, especially as I was dead tired, and he worked very hard for me to try and give me a rest and I feel his death very deeply indeed.

The post is just going, so I must hurry up with what I have to tell you .He was buried yesterday a hundred yards from where he fell. After he was killed I went through his pockets to send you back anything. As I was doing so a shell burst and knocked me and my orderly over and buried us, so I fear some of the few private personal effects that he had with him are lost. I know there was a small pig that he loved, but it was buried, also his watch. The orderly was taken straight to hospital, I shall go to see him today and find if he saved anything.

The only things I have were his identity disc and his cigarette case, which if you will allow me to, I am very anxious to keep till the end of the war, and if I get killed I will see it is returned to you. I fear this letter is very disjointed, but I've only just come out of the line. We have had the hardest time I have ever had and for once I feel rather shaken and most terribly sad.

With my love and my very deepest sympathies.

Yours very sincerely.

Percy Baltye.

PS I particularly want a photograph of Nigel if you would be kind enough to send me one. I will write again tomorrow. Just before he was killed, we were talking about home and other things, and his last words to me about one minute before he was killed were: "Thank God, Percy, we are out here, and not winning the war

The second of the three Newall brothers, Keith, was in the Royal Navy and survived the war. He had two children.

I'm not sure if there is any real connection between the Newall boys and the statue, maybe it was simply a local legend. When the Peace Memorial Hospital in Watford was demolished the statue was moved to a site close to the Town Hall.

Further research revealed a memorial to William Newall in Langleybury churchyard and it is dated 1922; it also commemorates the deaths of Nigel and Leslie. I guess that the Newall boys' parents moved to Langleybury after the war. Nigel is commemorated as missing on the Tyne Cot memorial and Leslie was buried in the military cemetery at Fleurbaix, near Armentieres but I cannot explain why their names don't appear on the memorial at Croxley.

Work on the Grand Junction Canal began in 1792. It linked up with the Oxford Canal and followed a line from Northampton, Leighton Buzzard and Berkhamsted and on through Cassiobury Park, Croxley Moor and Uxbridge to Brentford. The canal was opened in 1805 and that one event changed Croxley forever. It also served to make my childhood an adventurous one!

John Dickinson already had paper mills in the area before he decided to build another alongside the canal at Croxley Green. The construction started in 1828 and Dickinson appeased Lord Ebury who owned a nearby estate at Moor Park by creating a grand Egyptian façade for the building to improve the good lord's view of things. Paper production started at Croxley in 1830. Dickinson was an engineer, builder, architect and financier who founded a highly successful company which still exists today.

A view of the canal from where the Mill used to be.

Front view of Mill

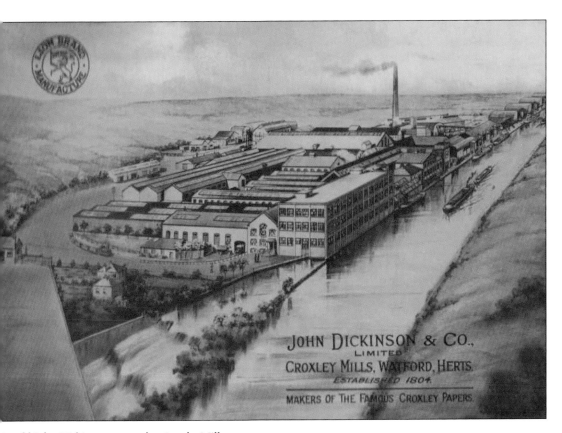

An old John Dickinson poster showing the Mill.

CROXLEY MILLS.
The Weir. Pure water for the manufacture of "Croxley Quality Papers."

The Weir's clear waters were used in the manufacture of Croxley Quality Papers

23

John Dickinson

John Dickinson was born in 1782 and he founded a giant business empire, eventually employing many thousands of people world-wide at its peak. He started his working life by training as a stationer in the City of London, becoming enrolled at Stationer's Hall in 1804 of which he eventually became Master for two years in 1857. A keen businessman and of an inventive practical nature, he must have been frustrated by the myriad of small paper mills with which he did business and realised that to be efficient he would have to have the whole process under his own control. At that time each mill was using its own methods of making each sheet of paper individually; a slow and expensive process often with variable quality.

He was the holder of many patents relating to paper and its use. His first was for a non smouldering paper for use in rifles, called Cartridge Paper; said to have been particularly helpful to Wellington's Peninsular campaign and at Waterloo by increasing the British firing rate whilst simultaneously reducing premature firing accidents. His next patent was for a means of making paper in a continuous sheet in what has become known as the Cylinder Mould machine. In an age of technical innovation, attempts had already been made to build a machine capable of the continuous manufacture of paper to replace the handmade techniques then used notably by the Frenchman, Henry Fourdrinier. Dickinson patented his own design in 1809. In that same year he found financial backing from George Longman. He was then able to purchase a former flour mill at Apsley which had already been converted to paper manufacture by the previous owner. The seller, a man called John Stafford, had been one of Dickinson's suppliers. Dickinson installed his own design of machinery at the mill.

Dickinson was involved with the development of the Penny Post, producing a paper containing silk threads for security purposes. He also patented a method of slitting paper with sharp bevelled wheels, still used on machines today and from which office guillotines in common use have evolved. In addition to his factories at Apsley and Nash he built two brand new mills at Home Park and Croxley in 1825 and 1828. Other sites in Manchester, Liverpool and elsewhere were created for distribution. Transportation of goods and coal occupied him in the early days and litigation with the Grand Junction Canal Company resulted in the re routing of the canal closer to his Apsley and Nash mills. He successfully tendered for the building work of locks and wharves required for the diversion in 1818.

During his career folded envelopes were developed and a wide variety of uses for paper and paper products explored. In 1858 John Dickinson retired, handing over the running of the business to his nephew, John Evans. Dickinson died in January 1869 having refused to call in his doctor on the grounds that he was too ill to see anyone!

The process consisted of a perforated cylinder of metal, with a closely fitting cover of finely woven wire, which revolved in a vat of wood pulp. The water from the vat was carried off through the axis of the cylinder, leaving the fibres of the wood pulp clinging to the surface of the wire. An endless web of felt passed through what was known as a 'couching roller' lying upon the cylinder that drew off the layer of pulp which, when dried, became paper. The mill brought prosperity to Croxley and evidence of Dickinson's legacy can still be seen in the village, particularly in the New Road area.

General photographs of Dickinson's Factory

The houses in Dickinson Square, just another of the many benefits the Mill brought to Croxley Green.

In 1887 Dickinson Papermakers Co-operative Society was formed. To begin with the store was in a cellar of the old Mill House. Various items were sold on a co-operative basis. The Co-op moved to number 5 Milestone Field, where Dickinson Square now stands. Later the Society was registered under the Friendly Societies Act as the Croxley Co-operative Society. George Kingham started out as 'Boy Assistant' and finished up as the manager.

The 1800s were times of great change for Croxley much of it brought about by John Dickinson's decision to build a paper mill but, as has always been the case during a period of change, many of the old ways still lingered. The name 'Smokey Hall Farm' shows up during this period but I can't really establish whether it was just one of those legends that exists in every town or village or even where 'Smokey Hall Farm' might have been. Some people suggest that it might have been a nickname for 'Stocky Hall Farm'. Whatever the explanation is we will probably never know.

When I started at Rickmansworth Grammar School we spent several hours picking stones from the new sports field and it seems that we were just following a tradition that dates back to the 1800s in Croxley! Picking stones from the fields was common practice up until the 1900s, the stones being used as material for the construction of the local roads. Not all farmers liked stone pickers on their land because some crops needed the moisture from the stones. As for me, I didn't enjoy stone picking but I did like the smell of the tar blocks which Dad used on the fire. The blocks came from roads in London which were being resurfaced

with more modern materials. Making toast in front of the open fire with those tar blocks crackling away is just one of the very best memories of my childhood.

The lane which runs across the canal bridge from Cassiobury Park, past West Herts Golf Club and down to Rousebarn Lane is probably one of the roads where Croxley stone was used. For us it was a great short cut from Watford back home after a night out at the 'flicks'. We called it 'The Stoney Lane'.

If the canal helped to bring prosperity to John Dickinson and his workers, it certainly proved to be a wonderful distraction to me and my friends when we were young. The area where the canal makes its way through Cassiobury Park rang to the sound of kids playing throughout the long summer holidays and we did manage to get into a few scrapes as well. I think that it might have been Dudley Withers who suggested that it would be fun to manipulate the lock gates in order to drain a stretch of the canal, the idea being to seek out some of the treasures we were certain must be lurking in the mud. Our efforts only revealed a couple of bike frames and so we headed home muddy but unbowed! Narrow boats still worked the canal when I was young and we would often cadge a ride from one lock to the next. Travelling at such a sedate speed gave us the opportunity to see the surrounding countryside in quite a different way and I still enjoy a walk along the towpath before making my way to Cassiobury Park.

CASSIOBURY PARK

The park is administered by Watford Borough Council but one cannot write about Croxley Green without mentioning one of the principal amenities in the area. The rivers Colne and Gade run through the park and there is still evidence of the old watercress beds where we paddled to cool ourselves after a robust game of 'cowboys and Indians'. These days there are swings and other constructions to keep the youngsters amused but my greatest memory of the park is when Flanagan's Fair came to town. I had my first glimpse of the female form at Flanagan's Fair! We had donated most of our pocket money to the man on the 'Hoopla' stall and the lady on the 'Hook a plastic duck' stand and were trying to make up our minds as to how best to invest what little cash we had left when I spotted a rather grubby man trying to tempt people into a tent. On investigation we found that the fellow was offering 'Artistic poses' being carried out by a young lady. He shouldn't have taken our money but he did and so we entered the gloomy tent and joined a curious group of about six men all staring at a small stage. The guy who had taken our money stood by the opening to the tent and, in between taking guilty glances to watch for the police, gave us a running commentary as to what the various poses taken by a large (and elderly) lady were supposed to depict. I have to say that it took many years before I could bring myself to look at the real Venus De Milo!

CASSIOBURY

Cassiobury is mentioned in the Domesday Book as belonging to the Abbey of St Albans. With the Dissolution of the Monasteries in 1539 King Henry VIII made himself Lord of the Manor and he sold the land to one Richard Morrison in 1545. Morrison began to build a large mansion; it was eventually completed by his son Charles.

Through marriage the estate passed to the Capel family. Lord Capel was executed in 1649 for his loyalty to Charles I. At the Restoration of the Monarchy his eldest son Arthur was created Earl of Essex and the estate was returned to the family. Arthur took on Hugh May to rebuild the house, incorporating the original Northwest wing. The first Earl also started developing the park, importing many exotic trees. In 1687 he was arrested and taken to the Tower for plotting to assassinate Charles II. In July of that year he was found with his throat cut.

In 1800 the 5th Earl commissioned James Wyatt to remodel the house but by 1902 the family was finding the house too expensive to keep and they moved out. In 1909 the 8th Earl sold 184 acres of the parkland to Watford Council for housing and a public park and the house was demolished in 1927. The grand staircase designed by Grinling Gibbons was removed to the Metropolitan Museum of Art in New York. Other materials from the house were used to restore Monmouth House in Watford High Street. In 1967 the entrance gates were demolished in order to widen the road, whoever made that decision will never be forgiven. There was a rumour that the gates actually finished up under the newly constructed road.

33

Cassiobury Gate, Watford

To the Woods!

Whippendell Woods are administered by Watford Council and they would probably not have approved of us kids using some of the branches of trees to fashion 'camps', bows and arrows, fishing rods and various other implements. As locals will be well aware, the woods are an absolute picture at bluebell time. More than 300 species of moth have been recorded in this wood, and there is an impressive avenue of lime trees leading from Cassiobury Park across West Herts Golf Course.

I am grateful to the Hertfordshire Countryside Management Services for permitting us to include the following details of walks that take in Whippendell Woods, Hassocks Wood, the Canalside and Cassiobury Park.

Coloured brochures with maps are available at various local Post Offices etc as well as from the Hertfordshire Countryside Management Team at County Hall.

These ancient woods once formed part of the Cassiobury Estate. Historically managed for timber, firewood and game, they are now open to the public for recreational enjoyment.

The woodland has been designated a Site of Special Scientific Interest (SSSI) due to its richness of wildlife, especially fungi and insects. The area is home to more than 270 species of plant, including 60 species of moss, and 10 species of liverwort.

During the hurricane of '87 and gales of '90 more than 2,500 trees were blown down or damaged throughout the wood. The open glades and woodland edge created by this are now home to many butterflies such as speckled wood, ringlet and holly blue. The woodland is also rich in bird life, including the tawny owl and sparrowhawk. Standing dead wood provides feeding and nesting sites for woodpeckers, with all three British species known to breed here.

As well as making the woods better for wildlife, continuing active management also makes them more attractive to people. Wide, open rides are more welcoming to walk along, and are less likely to become muddy during winter months. The route followed by this walk is surfaced and free from stiles and gates, allowing easy access throughout the year.

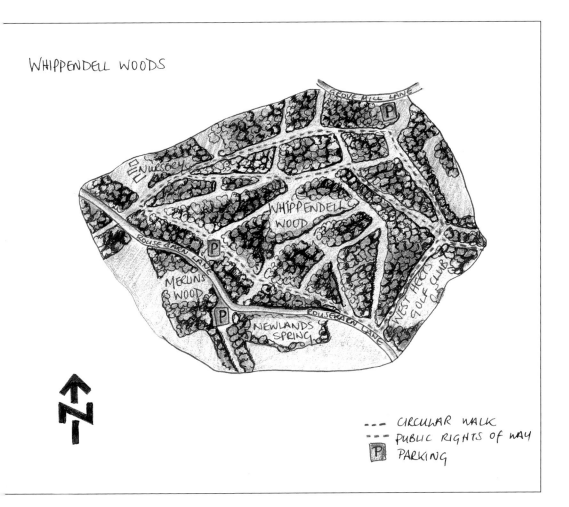

WHIPPENDELL WOODS

--- CIRCULAR WALK
--- PUBLIC RIGHTS OF WAY
P PARKING

WALK TWO - WOODLAND TRUST WOODS

This walk takes you on a tour of some of the small woodlands typical of southern Hertfordshire. Much of the area was previously designated a Site of Special Scientific Interest (SSSI), however felling of many large trees and destruction of the ground flora through cattle grazing resulted in the loss of this status.

Harrocks Wood is notable for the presence of coral root bittercress (Cardamine bulbifera). In spring this nationally rare flowering plant can be found growing mainly in the dappled light along path sides and woodland edges.

As the name suggests Dell Wood contains many dells or hollows, relics of previous use when the area was excavated to supply flints and gravel. Many examples of their use in construction can still be seen throughout the local area.

In 1986 the woods were bought by the Woodland Trust, and have since been brought back into active management. Traditionally hazel is cut near to the ground (coppiced) every seven to ten years, the 'stools' regrow giving a constant supply of wood used for hedgelaying, charcoal making and country crafts. The open areas created by coppicing receive more sunlight, allowing the ground flora to flourish. This in turn provides a valuable habitat attracting many birds and butterflies.

All stiles on this route have been replaced with kissing gates to allow easier access.

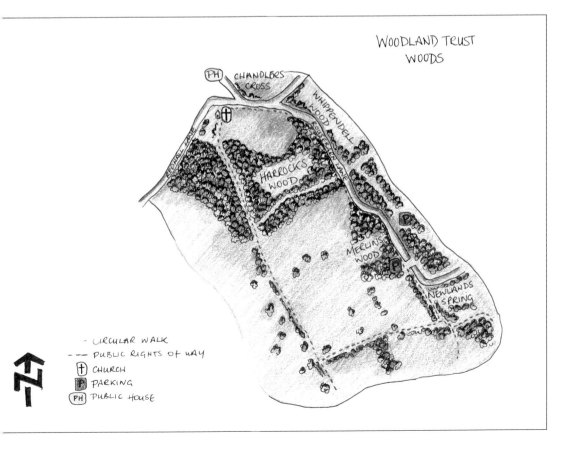

WOODLAND TRUST WOODS

- CIRCULAR WALK
--- PUBLIC RIGHTS OF WAY
☦ CHURCH
🄿 PARKING
(PH) PUBLIC HOUSE

A walk based along quiet lanes still little used by car traffic, this route takes you from the cool woodland of Whippendell, along the urban fringe of Croxley Green, and into the wide arable landscape beyond.

Follow Rousebarn Lane, a shady sunken lane bordered by steep hedge banks. These ancient woodland boundaries are lined with mature oak and ash trees. Now designated Heritage Roadside Verges, they are unadulterated by modern mowing and flailing techniques, giving rise to a varied covering of mosses, lichens and flowering plants. Shade and damp are ever-present giving rise to a fine array of fungi throughout the year, look closely and you may see russulas and ceps growing throughout the hot summer months.

The pond at Little Green now holds little water during the summer; despite this it is home to a variety of attractive plants like water forget-me-not. Such seasonal ponds are of great importance in the English landscape but during the twentieth century their numbers dwindled through neglect or in-filling, reducing breeding sites for frogs, newts and toads. From this point the walk enters typical Hertfordshire arable farmland where wide-open fields are peppered with small copses and remnant hedgerows. The character of this landscape changes constantly with the seasons, as crops such as wheat and forage maize mature and are harvested.

This walk contains both gates and stiles.

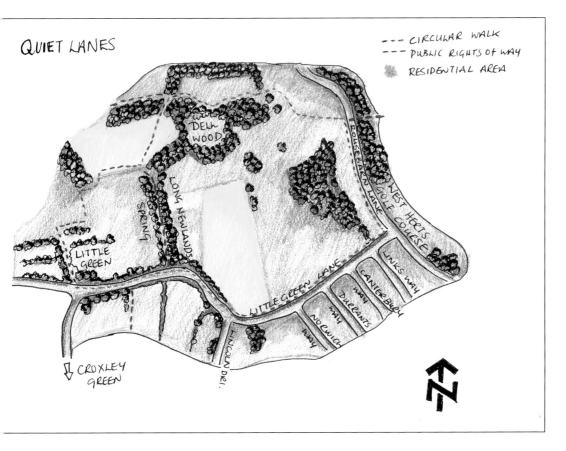

WALK FOUR - THE GRAND UNION TO CROXLEY GREEN

This walk links the historic Cassiobury Estate, Whippendell Woods and Croxley Green on a longer walk along the Grand Union Canal.

The Grand Junction Canal, as it was originally known, was developed to serve the fast growing paper industry in the valleys of the Rivers Gade, Chess and Colne. Built to link the Thames at Brentford with the Midlands at Braunston, this section was opened as far as Hemel Hempstead in 1797. To avoid the delay and expense of tunnelling through high ground it was necessary to divert the planned course of the canal through Cassiobury Estate. The Earl of Essex, who occupied the estate at that time, demanded that the towpath be switched to the western side of the canal to allay his fears of poaching. He was further compensated £15,000, leading to an increased toll of 1 penny per ton being enforced on all goods passing through this section of canal.

A fleet of nearly 400 craft traded along the canal until the end of the Second World War, when the canals system was nationalised in 1948.

Whilst walking along Croxley Green keep a look out for the cattle trough. Erected by the Metropolitan Drinking Fountain and Cattle Trough Association, it included a push button drinking fountain and separate dog trough. Only five examples of this design now remain within Hertfordshire.

This walk contains some gates and stiles.

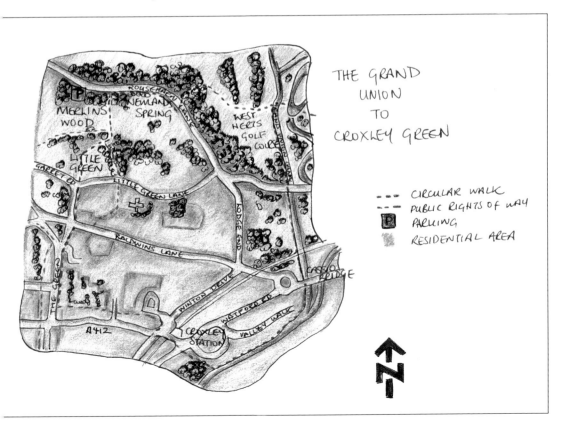

THE GRAND
UNION
TO
CROXLEY GREEN

--- CIRCULAR WALK
--- PUBLIC RIGHTS OF WAY
P PARKING
RESIDENTIAL AREA

Cassiobury Park has been awarded Grade II status within the National Register of Historic Parks and Gardens. The park boasts 190 acres of undulating, picturesque landscape, influenced by figures such as Le Notre and Humphrey Repton. The River Gade meanders through the western part of the park known as Cassiobury Wood, along with the Grand Union Canal. Other features include veteran trees, wetland, former watercress beds and old pasture.

More recent attractions within the park include a children's play area, large paddling pools with refreshments kiosk, along with bowls, tennis and croquet pavilions.

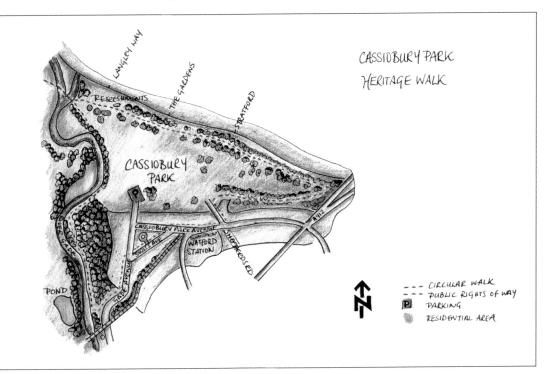

CASSIOBURY PARK HERITAGE PROJECT

This Project has been developed to bring the park's rich cultural and ecological heritage to life, with local schools helping to develop an interpretation strategy. This walk will form the basis of a 'Museum without Walls', to include text and art based pieces. When completed, the refurbishment of the Tea Pavilion, and creation of a visitor centre will provide a focal point to the park.

ACCESS

The main entrance from Gade Avenue provides vehicular access and parking facilities. Pedestrians can also enter the park from Shepherds Road, Rickmansworth Road, Stratford Way, Langley Way and The Gardens.

This walk is largely surfaced and contains no stiles or gates.

Scots Hill

The bottom of Scots Hill is where Croxley Green begins if you approach it from Rickmansworth. And I have to tell you that I recall the hill as being much steeper than it is today! Certainly in winter it was not uncommon for buses and other heavy vehicles to become stuck on the hill due to ice and snow.

I was always aware that the British Friesian Cattle Society had their headquarters on Scots Hill at Scotsbridge (or Scotch Bridge) House but was never sure as to what it did! Well, it merged with the Holstein Breed Society in 1999 and the headquarters of Holstein UK are still at the bottom of the hill. The house was occupied by Admiral the Hon. Josceline Percy between 1827 and 1856. The Admiral is buried at West Hyde; he led quite a life and his obituary in *The Times* states: "The gallant deceased was Lieutenant of the Diadem at the reduction of the Cape in 1806, Captain of the Hotspur in action with the French flotilla on the coast of Normandy in 1811. He was Commander in Chief on the Cape of Good Hope station for three years and subsequently Commander in Chief at the Nore until 1854". He also had a mountain named after him. In 1842 a British expedition led by Sir Jarvis Ross discovered the mountain on Joinville Island in the Antarctic.

The old greenhouse

A dog's grave in the gardens

Front entrance to Scotsbridge House

Bridge over River Chess

The records show that there has been a house on the site since 1692 and that it was rebuilt around 1850. In the 1920s the house was owned by a Mr. Campbell Walker, who was a member of the 'Johnny Walker' whisky family and oddly enough the house was sold on to a Mr. Grant of Grant's 'Steadfast Whisky'!

Obviously the house was named because of its proximity to Scots Hill and I must admit that I never really gave any thought as to why the hill is so named, but two explanations have been offered through my research. It could be that the name is a derivation of the word 'Skote', an ancient word meaning lookout point, or 'Scotch' which was a block used to stop the wheels of coaches slipping backwards down a hill. A map of 1777 shows the spelling as 'Scotch Hill'. And just to prove that in matters of a historical nature there are as many theories as there are people, a legal document dating back to the time of Edward II reveals that the family of one Simon le Skote lived in the area. So maybe old Simon was a lookout?

Apart from Josceline Percy, several other notables lived there, including Lord Peterborough between 1746 and 1761.

The mill is on the other side of the road to Scotsbridge House and, although its history is not all that clear, we do know that reference is made to a mill on the site in 1757. In that year the fulling mill was turned into a paper mill by Thomas Child. From that time the mill had several owners and became a corn mill again and then reverted to paper making! During the early 1930s the mill appeared in several British films, probably as the result of Metro Goldwyn Mayer buying an interest in the building. Before the outbreak of the Second World War the film company moved their offices from London to the mill. When the film company moved out, rumours of a ghostly nature began. People reported hearing strange footsteps, voices and coughing noises and also smelling perfume. A local priest, Father Lemmon, was asked to exorcise the ghosts but reports continued until the premises were completely gutted to allow for refurbishment. The mill is now a restaurant and several of the original features remain. The river runs through the building and one can see 'fish steps' which were constructed to allow the fish to travel upstream.

Education in the Broadest Sense

At the top of Scots Hill stands Rickmansworth School, formerly Rickmansworth Grammar School and a place that offered yours truly education on the days I chose to attend. Opposite the school was Luxton's shop, which was much more interesting than the school because it offered us youngsters the last chance to pick up some confectionery before crossing the road and entering the hallowed hall of learning. I use the words 'pick up' deliberately because some kids often failed to pay Mr. Luxton, naturally I was not one of them! Opposite the church which stands on the corner of the green, there was a small café and baker's shop where penny buns could be purchased and, if you could give the teacher the slip, a young fellow could use his dinner money to purchase egg and chips and eat them alongside the lorry drivers. The school itself was custom built and brand new when I arrived along with the first intake (there were second year pupils as well but they had attended Clarendon School for a year before transferring).

Education was never really high on my list of priorities and no one was more surprised than I was when I passed the exams that took me to grammar school. To be honest, there were a couple of other people who were more surprised than me. Mr. Worthy, the headmaster of Little Green Lane Junior Mixed, told my mum that he had asked for the results to be checked again when he saw them and his good lady wife who was my class teacher agreed. Anyway, I did pass and I did attend, on occasions and these occasions were noted by my form teachers and used in evidence some years later.

It was a good school and they were a great bunch of teachers, it was just that I already had a job with Bill the greengrocer that paid real money. Bill worked for a firm called Berridges from Watford and his patch was Croxley Green. When I first became aware of Bill he delivered greengrocery by horse and cart and the horse was also the source of food for the roses! Bill took me on as 'Saturday Boy' when I was eleven and I worked for him until I left school. We started our round in Links Way and continued to the very end of that road, then turned around to knock on customers' doors in Richmond Way and Warwick Way. At the last call Bill would enter a customer's house for a cup of tea and leave me to make up a sack of fruit and vegetables to take home to my mum. He also gave me ten shillings for my day's work, which was a fortune then. I had a daily paper round as well so you can appreciate how school sort of got in the way of my entrepreneurial activities.

All good things have to come to an end and it came to an end for me when the chairman of the school governors opened his front door one morning to find a young man in Rickmansworth Grammar School uniform delivering his laundry! Colonel Goad informed the headmaster, who informed my mum that it was felt best that I should leave school and get a job. So I left school one year earlier than my grammar school mates, told Bill that I couldn't work for him anymore, chucked in my paper round, informed Rickmansworth Laundry that I couldn't assist their driver anymore either, and got a job at Burton's the Tailors in Watford.

Courtesy of Croxley Stitchers

E.C.2/51.

HERTFORDSHIRE COUNTY COUNCIL
Telephone: Hertford 3131. Extension 137.

J.H. Newsom, M.A.
County Education Officer.

Education Department,
County Hall,
Hertford.

May, 1954.

Dear Sir or Madam,

Selection for Secondary Education - Examination 1954.

1. I am writing to tell you that the course of secondary education for which your child appears to be suitable having regard to the child's school record and work in connection with the recent examination is that of a secondary grammar school and that it has therefore been decided to transfer the child to the

RICKMANSWORTH
GRAMMAR SCHOOL

at the beginning of the Autumn Term subject to your entering into the County form of undertaking mentioned in paragraph 4 below.

2. No tuition fees will be payable and books will be provided.

3. The County Council will be prepared to pay the travelling expenses of any child who lives more than three miles from the school and arrangements will be made for the issue of railway season or bus term tickets as the case may be. In accordance with the provisions of the Education Act, 1944, the County Council may pay maintenance allowances on behalf of necessitous children over compulsory school leaving age i.e. from the beginning of the school term following their 15th birthday. Forms of application may be obtained from the Divisional Education Officer.

4. The curriculum of the grammar school is designed to provide a sound all-round education over a course of at least five or six years leading to the examination for the General Certificate of Education. It is, therefore, of little use for children to enter a Grammar School for less than this period, and before your child is admitted to the school you will be asked to enter into an undertaking to keep the child in attendance at least until the end of the school year following his or her 16th birthday, unless the child is granted exemption for any adequate reason such as your removal from the district or unless the child does not appear to be profiting from a grammar school education.

5. The full benefits of the grammar school curriculum can normally be obtained only by completing the course in the sixth form, and the County Council hope that if your child's progress is satisfactory you will make every effort to keep the child at the school until then.

6. If you approve of your child's transfer to the grammar school the enclosed form of undertaking should be completed, signed, and sent immediately to the Head Master or Mistress of the Grammar School.

Yours faithfully,

J.H. Newsom.

County Education Officer.

To the Parent.
Enc. (Form E.9/45).

Above is the letter that galvanised my mum into taking out Provident Cheques to pay for the items listed here ➤

SCHOOL UNIFORM — BOYS

The school uniform, in dark green, grey and maroon, has been approved by the Governors, and is obtainable from the following firms :—

Andrew Forbes Ltd., 5 Queens Road, Watford
(Tel. Watford 3511)

Wheatleys Ltd., Odeon Parade, Rickmansworth
(Tel. Rickmansworth 3202)

The list below shows what we consider necessary for every child. All articles of clothing should be clearly marked with the owner's name.

School Uniform	Approximate Prices
Dark green cap, including badge	7/6
Dark green blazer, including badge	50/- to 60/-
Grey Shirt	
Maroon tie (Tootal shade 12)	4/-
Medium grey flannel shorts or trousers	
Dark green V-neck pullover	
Grey socks	
Black shoes	
Brown sandals or house shoes with crêpe soles and heels	
Navy blue raincoat	
Gloves—leather or grey wool	
Woollen scarf—dark green, with maroon and grey stripes	

Winter Games Wear

(from Wheatleys, or Wrens, 46 High St., Watford)

White gym shorts (Bukta)
White socks
White gym shoes with crêpe soles
Rugby football boots (black)
Rugby shorts (navy blue, Bukta)
Rugby shirt (one dark green, reversible)
Rugby socks (dark green)
Sweater (white, V neck, long sleeves)

Summer Games Wear

White shirt
White flannels (long or short)

School brochure

51

A windmill was built at the top of Scots Hill in 1830 but there is some evidence of earlier windmills. Sam Parrot had a mill at Croxley in 1693 and mention is made of Mill Field near to 'Jaggerts Hill' in 1766 (perhaps this is the hill I knew as 'Jacotts Hill').

Probably the name most associated with this mill is that of the Holloway family. Ephraim Holloway was already living at the mill when he purchased it in September 1877. The 1830s version was a brick tower and had a cap with sails and a fantail. The sails were later lost in a gale and steam power was employed following that event. The windmill was a warden post during the Second World War and had an air raid siren. After the war it became a private house.

Ephraim Holloway was a well known sportsman in the area and his son Jim became known as a demon bowler. He captained the Croxley cricket team when games were played on a field opposite the present site of the Red House.

THE GOOD OLD VILLAGE GREEN

Courtesy of Croxley Stitchers

These days a village green is somewhere for people to have fun and to relax but it wasn't always so. It is difficult to pinpoint the exact origins of village greens but most date back to medieval times. In those early days a green's main purpose was probably to enclose livestock and a pond was usually to be found in the area. The enclosure served two purposes. Firstly it would defend the villager's livestock from both animal predators and human ones as well. It would also have been used to keep in stray cattle. Later on village water pumps would be found on the green along with whipping posts and stocks, but inevitably they would also have been used as a centre of celebration for the community. May Day was celebrated on Croxley Green when I was a kid and I have no doubt that it would have been so many years before I tripped the light fantastic around the Maypole! Archaeologists now believe that some village greens do not in fact mark the original site of a village but they are more likely to be the area that was first cleared as people moved from an earlier site and this may be the case with Croxley Green.

In any event the green was a valuable resource for a community and several have remained pretty much unchanged over the years. It is to the credit of the residents of Croxley that their green is well preserved.

The Green was also the site of an annual fair in the month of August and on three Sundays in July Cherry Fairs were held. Stalls would be set up close to Stone's Orchard and Parrots. My brother George used to help out at Stone's Orchard and he once nearly settled for poor old Mr. Stone! The gentleman kept an old muzzle loader gun which he used to scare the birds and young George was entrusted with the weapon one day. He had never really handled such a thing and rammed the gunpowder down too tight, the gun failed to go off and Mr. Stone irritably snatched the thing back and pulled the trigger. The gun exploded into a thousand pieces and when the smoke cleared Mr. Stone's face appeared, covered in a black substance. George was never allowed to use the gun again.

"In Hertfordshire at Croxley Green, Stone's Community Orchard is a 1.4 hectare relic of an orchard once nearly four times as large. Such orchards formed an important element of the local economy a century ago. Cherry Sundays were fairs held in July in many orcharding villages in south-west Hertfordshire and combined picking and sales in local orchards including Stone's. Today, new saplings of the dark Carroon (Kerroon) and Hertfordshire Black cherries, as well as local apple varieties and plums, stand among the still flowering ancient giants that Walter Stone may have planted".

From the Common Ground Book of Orchards, 2000.

The orchard is now a public area where people can enjoy a stroll, sit in the sunshine and bless their good luck that they live in a place that deals in preserving this kind of history.

Over the years farmers had grazing rights on the green and it was as the result of working for a local farmer that I believe my brother George first took an interest in agriculture. He spent many happy hours working at Killingdown Farm for Joe Foster and cherished a dream of becoming a farmer for a while, I think, that was just before he ran away to Australia!

My sister June told me that she and the young man destined to become her husband used to earn some extra money weeding in Mr. Foster's fields. It seems that her fiancé had a disagreement with the farmer because June was paid less than he was.

Entrance to Killingdown Farm

Courtesy of Croxley Stitchers

Providence Hall is one of the oldest houses on the green and it stands alongside the entrance to Croxley Guild of Sport, which used to be Dickinson's Sports Field. The wrought iron gates were given to the cricket club by a Mr. Morland who used to allow them to play in his park. I mentioned the fact that most greens would have a pond and, at one time, Croxley Green had five! 'Stones', 'Streeters', 'Coxhills', 'Little Green' and 'Robinsons'.

Courtesy of Croxley Stitchers

55

Another house on the Green has associations with the Pilgrim family. 'Campions' (now known as 'Crossely Wylde') was once the home of dog trainer Barbara Woodhouse and my dad worked for the good lady for many years. As a kid I was scared of Mrs. Woodhouse. She had a very imposing character to say the least and was completely absorbed with her dogs 'Juno' and 'Jynte'. When she wasn't working with her beloved canines, Mrs. Woodhouse spent a good deal of time breathing up the noses of cows and horses! She is said to have developed this unusual method for training animals whilst she was living in Argentina. She wrote books about her dogs and also made films, and photos of my dad in various guises appeared in a couple of the books and he also 'starred' in some of the films as well. In later life the Woodhouse family moved across the road into a new house also called 'Campions'. Barbara Woodhouse had several careers. She was born in Ireland and moved to England with her mother when her father died. I don't know much about her early life but I do know that she went to Argentina for a while and that it was when she married and moved to Croxley that her animal training methods really took off. She was a very determined lady and she set about writing books and making films with her own production company. She managed to gain the support and services of several well known personalities such as Richard Dimbleby for her projects. Her early films were *Trouble With Junia* (1967), *A Star is Made* (1963), *Juno Makes Friends* (1957), *Trouble for Juno* (1956), *and Love me Love my Dog* (1954) and it is a fair bet that Arthur George Pilgrim, my dad, appeared in those made in the 1950s. Barbara was born in 1910 and died in 1988 from a stroke but not before relaunching her career both in this country and in the United States. I didn't like her, my dad did and you have to admire someone who worked so hard at promoting herself throughout her life. Why didn't I like her? Because she was bossy and intimidating to a young lad like me and her bloody dogs bit me on several occasions!

Crossely Wylde

The author's father rewarding Juno.

In the winter of 1991 two 'young, thrusting lads' (their description not mine), responded to an advert in the *'Resident'* magazine. Basically the Revels committee was diminishing and needed new blood and ideas. The 'lads' turned up at a Croxley hostelry to offer their services, took a few drinks on board and became involved in something they hadn't really bargained for.

Basically the problem was that the Revels, whilst being popular, would wind up at about four o' clock on the day and people would go home. The new recruits decided on a new policy – 'Pushball'. Naturally it was necessary to partake of several meetings and several pints of beer in friendly circumstances but the principle was established, a 'Pushball' competition would be the finale for the Revels. Mark Saxon (who still insists that he be referred to as a young and thrusting individual along with Barry Grant, and believe me, I have met them) showed the lads a tatty brochure from a Croydon based firm who would be prepared to supply a fully inflated ball that stood five feet tall. I'm not quite sure exactly what the rules were but the group employed the services of Harvey Road School and training began. Several children and parents joined in enthusiastically and, despite the odd injury, everyone agreed that 'Pushball' was a winner. Sixteen years on the rules are (pretty much) agreed and the game is a fitting finale to the Revels. It has to be said that local entrepreneur Peter Grand helped out when hiring a ball became a little expensive and he supplied one at a not inconsiderate cost. So there you have it, 'Pushball' is aggressive, spooky, involves grandmas and grandads, kids of all ages, and for all I know, local vicars, priests, farmers, the family dog, various Parish Councillors and you if you fancy it. It sounds like an altogether fitting and exciting conclusion to the Croxley Revels, long may it be so. For more details of the Revels take a look at the website www.croxleyrevels.co.uk But be warned, you have to be young and thrusting!

Pushball

CROXLEY HOUSE

The house is built on the site of earlier buildings known sometimes as 'Harry Smiths' Harwoods or Harwells which existed before 1620. It was then owned by William Sonsomer and was given to Mary, who was the wife of Richard Thompson of Watford. In her will Mary bequeathed the house to her grandchild, Mary, in 1653. Descendants of Mary Thompson called Tuffen took over the house in 1737 and Richard Tuffen sold it to Solomon Andremin of Watford, who then sold it to Thomas, Lord Hyde in 1767. He became Earl of Clarendon in 1778. The Earl extended the house and built the wall which still surrounds the property today.

From then on the house was owned by Thomas, the second Earl followed by Humphrey Cornwall Woolrych, his son. In 1871 the property was inherited by William Richard Woolrych whose great aunt was Miss Mary Bentley. The last of the Woolrych family was Colonel Woolrych. In the 1920s Colonel and Mrs Woolrych went to live at Parrots, a farmhouse near the Green.

The aforementioned Miss Mary Bentley was a wealthy woman and in 1834 she had The Grove built on the corner of the Green at the top of Baldwins Lane. It was at The Grove some years later that my father Arthur George Pilgrim went to work! Great Aunt Mary also had a row of cottages built where All Saints' church stands today. The cottages were known as 'Penny Row' because they were let to elderly people at a small annual rent. Following the First World War these cottages were renamed 'Heroes Terrace' and were rented by veterans for a shilling a week.

During the Second World War Croxley House was leased to St Dunstan's. In her history of Croxley House, Mildred Green tells how a resident of New Road talked about taking some of the residents of the house to the cinema in Rickmansworth. Les Rollett says that when they came out of the 'pictures' it was so foggy that the buses had stopped running. When they arrived back at the house the matron wanted to know how they had managed to get home and Les said, "We held hands and the boys got me home". For those who don't know, St Dunstan's was a charity for the blind! The WRVS purchased the house in 1949 and it is now a pleasant retirement home.

Main view of House

The author musing in the grounds

In the grounds of Croxley House there is evidence of the ingenuity required in bygone days in order to obtain water. The set of wooden cog wheels were hand operated and were used to raise water some two hundred and fifty feet. This construction probably dates back to the 1770s when the house was built.

Wellhouse

Cogs' wellhouse

The face in a wall at Croxley House has been the subject of questions on the world wide web as to its origin.

Situated in the walled garden is a nursery owned by P&D Gardening. 'Ring the bell for assistance!'

Two acres of land called 'Le Copdethorne' was granted to the Hospital de Pre at Saint Albans by the monastery in 1194 so people have been living in this area of Croxley Green for quite a while. I suspect that the cost of living there has gone up a bit over the years though!

There used to be a blacksmith's shop at the end of the road near the green and it seems that building really began in earnest during the very early 1900s. Copthorne Road was a 'no go area' when I was a kid. Naturally we failed to observe this unwritten rule and used what was, in those days, a private road, as a short cut to Rickmansworth. I can't be sure but I think that the chairman of the governors for Rickmansworth Grammar School lived in the road or certainly nearby. If that is the case then it would have been on this hallowed ground that a fifteen year old was 'nabbed' playing truant and given his marching orders from the school. So perhaps the residents got their own back for all the years I had used the road as a short cut.

The house called 'Chess Side' in Copthorne Road was once the home of Mr. Ingleby Oddie who wrote a book called *Inquest – A Coroner Looks Back* which, I have to admit, is not a title to inspire me. Nevertheless Samuel Ingleby Oddie did choose to write on a subject he knew well. As Coroner for several London districts he held many inquests that attracted public interest. Among the more high profile cases were the so called Charing Cross trunk murder and the assassination of Field Marshal Sir Henry Wilson. He also officiated at the inquest into the deaths of the people who died in the R.101 air crash. During his latter years Ingleby Oddie investigated deaths on the road and he made several suggestions as to what should appear in The Highway Code. Another fascinating fact about this man is that he was a good friend of Sir Arthur Conan Doyle. Doyle was much interested in the art of boxing and wrote a book entitled *The Croxley Master and Other Tales of the Ring*. I like to think that although the book does not really describe in any way Croxley Green, Doyle's friendship with the coroner influenced the title of the book, which in fact was made into a film in 1921. Taking my theory one step further, could Ingleby Oddie have been the inspiration for Doctor Watson? Probably not but you never know - after all research shows that there was a Mr. Watson living in Copthorne at the same time as Ingleby Oddie! Incidentally Ingleby Oddie was pretty active locally as well, he was a member of Rickmansworth District Council from at least 1911 to 1932 and Chairman of Rickmansworth UDC from 1918 to 1932. It is also worth mentioning that the august gentleman was a member of the team which prosecuted Dr. Crippen.

Another distinguished resident of Copthorne Road was Dr. C. E. R. Bruce who is credited for the discovery of lightning on the Sun in 1941. I can't explain his theories because I don't understand them, but there is no doubt that the gentleman was (and still is) revered in scientific circles.

In the 1930s he seems to have devoted more time to the running of the hockey and cricket clubs at Chalfont St. Peter, of both of which he was Captain and Secretary, than he did stargazing. Dr Bruce died in 1979. Briefly his Electrical Discharge theory goes like this:

"The surfaces of stars can be explained as lightning discharges which are observed in the atmosphere of the Earth". But I guess you already knew that!

How Copthorne Road Developed

I am indebted to Mike Collins of the Copthorne Road Residents Association for the following information. I have mentioned how Copthorne probably got its name but Mike explains that there is evidence that Palaeolithic man was living in the area some two hundred and fifty thousand years ago and that stone age tools have been found in his garden which date back over four thousand years. In the fifteenth century the manor was conveyed to the Abbot of St Albans and later to the Crown. As I have already mentioned Dr John Caius bought it from the Crown in 1557 and he gave it to Gonville and Caius College including most but not all of what is now Copthorne Road. The earliest map of the area is dated 1776 where Copthorne Road is shown with the fields behind Copthorne Wood pretty much as they are today.

Up until 1860 the colleges of Caius and Gonville were not allowed to sell off any of the land but the statutes were altered and the decision to develop the area of Copthorne Road was probably taken at around this time. In 1880 the top end of the road was sold to Mr. Woods who owned the Durrants Estate. Various pieces of land changed hands from around 1879 and slowly the road began to take shape.

COPTHORNE COTTAGES

Courtesy of Croxley Stitchers

In his history of Copthorne Road Mike Collins mentions a Baroness de Bertouch who lived in Copthorne Road and says "whoever she was". That is like a red rag to a bull, Mike, so here is what Margaret Ward and I have been able to find out.

'De Bertouch' is a Danish title, we think, and there was a Beatrice Caroline Elmslie who married Montagu F.W. de Bertouch in 1882 in Kensington. She was born about 1859.

'Beatrice Caroline Baroness de Bertouch' died aged 72, 8 Jan 1931 'of 9 The Mount, Caversham, Berks, and formerly of The Warren, De La Warr Road, Bexhill on Sea, Sussex'. There wasn't an obituary in The Times, only a legal notice asking for any creditors to get in touch.

She was mentioned in The Times on several occasions between 1900 and 1910 and then it all goes quiet. Nothing specific, just her name listed as attending functions – 1900 at the opening of the Women's Exhibition at Earls Court, 1901 at the AGM of the Actors' Orphanage Fund, 1901 at a meeting of the Society of Women Journalists, 1902 with the Baron at a garden party in honour of some Japanese Rear Admiral, 1904 an advert for the Father Ignatius book, 1908 her name in an advert for the Women's School of Journalism and Secretarial Training, 1910 with the Baron at a dinner of the Poetry Recital Society.

The reference to the Women's School of Journalism and Secretarial Training is interesting because we know that the Baroness wrote the words to a song entitled 'My Ladye's Garden' and that she wrote a book about Father Ignatius this evidence would seem to place our Baroness in the company of writers. We couldn't find any other references to the lady between 1912 and the time of her death in 1931 which is a bit odd because we know that she was living in Croxley Green in 1914 at a house called 'The Oak', maybe she moved there at the outbreak of the First World War and simply 'kept her head down' for the duration?

Margaret Ward did come up with another fascinating fact. The Baroness was living at 7 Hereford Square, London in 1908 and at 27 Scarsdale Villas, London in 1911 & 1912. (She had a telephone, so she appears in very early telephone directories!) Margaret's great aunt was housekeeper to the Watsons, who lived at 19 Scarsdale Villas at the same time. They were writers/artists and she knows that they were prone to giving dinner parties that included politicians etc. So Margaret's great-aunt Jane probably cooked dinner for the Baroness one evening! This information perhaps also backs up the literary connections we found.

Artichoke
Coach+Horses
Duke of York
Fox+Hounds
George+Dragon
Halfway House
Plough
Red House
Rose
Sportsman
Two Bridges

Courtesy of Croxley Stitchers

I am reliably informed that my brother in law Joe O'Mahoney's relations ran the Coach and Horse on the Green for a while. I remember it as a rather pleasant place where a young man could take the odd glass of Barley Wine! The records show that one William Southam paid a tithe in 1774 on the Coach and Horses and until around 1828 the place was run by Lydia Southam.

In 1819 a Society of Good Fellowship was formed at the Artichoke on The Green at Croxley. These societies were common at the time and basically they made provision for people who became blind or lame or who suffered some other form of incapacity.

Many years later the pub supplied us kids with considerable entertainment when the landlord purchased a parrot (or it could have been a cockatoo). On sunny days the bird was placed in his cage outside the pub and we would teach it to swear, although, if truth be known, it had already received some coaching from the pub regulars. The innkeeper in 1756 was one Thomas White and from 1773 to 1852 the Austins, Arthur, Sarah and Joseph, managed the pub successively. In days of yore customers would challenge those from the Coach and Horses to a game of quoits.

When David and I visited (purely in the cause of historical accuracy you understand) the landlady showed us a picture on the wall and related a strange story. She explained that the picture of a Scotsman complete with kilt is said to show one Mr. McPeters who, having travelled as far south as Rickmansworth during the Jacobite Revolution, was involved in a battle, caught and hanged on Croxley Green! The good lady also claimed that the man's ghost haunts the Artichoke and that she has seen him on several occasions. No problem, she's licensed for spirits.

My 'big brother' George frequented the Fox and Hounds during his youth along with his friends Peter McBride and a certain 'Dodger Beaumont' (who played some games for Watford F.C.). George Banting bought the land on which, it is assumed, he built the pub around 1866. In the 19th century an inquest was held there into the death of Alfred Ragnell, whose body had been found in the nearby canal. In George's day the pub was run by Frank Tyson and I believe that Frank's daughter Brenda was a source of interest to my brother!

Fox and Hounds

The Halfway House once stood literally halfway between Watford and Rickmansworth. It was pulled down in the 1950s when road widening took place. Before my time, Benskin's beers were loaded on barges bound for London from a wharf at the Halfway House unfortunately I was unable to find a photograph of the pub.

Originally the Duke of York in Watford Road was called the Gladstone Arms, which was built around 1870 and renamed in 1900. At the time of writing the building is up for sale, presumably, for redevelopment.

The Plough and the George and Dragon no longer exist. They stood at the top of Scots Hill close to where the Sportsman is today.

The Plough

The Dragon

The Sportsman was owned by Thomas Blackwell in 1838 and was not really recognised as a public house until 1870 when Benjamin Rockliff is noted as the owner. These days the pub has a lively clientele on certain nights and the Croxley Needlecrafters and other groups meet there regularly.

The Sportsman

The Two Bridges

I remember the Two Bridges on Watford Road being built. It was opened in 1954 by Benskin's Watford Brewery who had purchased the cottages on the site in 1934. They certainly took their time in replacing the Halfway House! The above photograph is of the built the way it is today.

Some Ways a Young Lad Could Make Some Extra Cash

Our visit to the Two Bridges prompted memories of Hygienic Dairies which stood just behind where the pub is now. Memory plays strange games as you get older so if I have got this information wrong I will be pleased to hear from you. The dairies employed two milkmen both named Fred and they delivered the milk by horse and cart. The Fred who I worked for as a kid had perfect hearing and used to meet up with a lady from another dairy who latterly used one of the new fangled electric vehicles. If I couldn't get work with good hearing Fred I offered my services to the other Fred, who definitely didn't hear too well. Poor hearing Fred had something of a temper but the money was the same so I put up with it. How well I remember the smell of horse! The first job in the morning was to tidy the stable, then hitch up the horse to the beautifully signwritten cart.

Just a lick and spit from Hygienic Dairies was Standen's shop situated on Watford Road. Mr. Standen sold tobacco, confectionary, newspapers and bottles of pop (to the uninitiated, pop means drinks like American Cream Soda, Tizer and Lemonade). There was also money to be made by working for Mr. Standen. Firstly, one could deliver newspapers and get paid. Secondly, delivering newspapers gave a small boy access to the shed where the empty pop bottles were kept. Access to the shed meant that it was possible to remove a couple of empty bottles and to 'return' them to the shop later in the day for the deposit cash of one penny. Mr. Standen also had a forsythia bush in his garden and that bush was used to supply a bunch of flowers for Mother's Day! Next to Standen's was Stan Pike's shop. Stan sold all manner of goods from washing powder to cheese and he also had a band that played at various local venues.

This is where Standen's and Pike's used to be on Watford Road.

GENERAL GROCERS
PROVISION MERCHANTS
GREENGROCERY

PIKES STORES

Watford Road Post Office
Croxley Green

Deliveries   Watford
Daily   2808

I think that 'Bertie' Brandon and his wife lived at number 1 Winton Drive and they had a grocery 'round' and a shed at the side of the house where all of his supplies were stored. 'Bertie' was a good friend of my dad and they used to go to the greyhound racing at Vicarage Road, Watford together and also enjoyed a regular punt on the horses. This was in the days before betting shops, when bookmaking was pretty dodgy business. My dad was barred by a local 'bookie' because he was winning too much! Dad enjoyed a bit of a gamble and although he always kept the exact amount of his winnings a secret from my mum, he made sure that everyone in the family benefited. I well remember Dad winning what was in those days a substantial amount of money on Vernon's Football Pools. He bought a new bike to get to and from work, a garden shed and a fountain pen! The new bike turned out to be a bit of a curse during its first week of use. By the time of his pools win my father had taken a job as a nightwatchman at Lapointe's in Watford. On his way to work he had to negotiate the new traffic lights at the bottom of Baldwins Lane at the intersection with Watford Road. It appears that Dad allowed the front wheel of his brand new bike to cross the white line at the traffic lights. The local 'Bobby' espied this dangerous and illegal act and attempted to charge my father with the heinous crime. Dad didn't take too kindly to the policeman's intervention and pushed him out of the way. My mother was mortified when Dad appeared in court and the *Watford Observer* reported the incident with the headline "Out of my way, says cyclist". Oh how times have changed.

There's a roundabout at the bottom of Baldwins Lane these days where my dad committed his dastardly deed!

The railway bridge on Baldwins Lane was where the local pigeons perched, we used to sprint under the bridge to avoid being spotted by the birds.

These shops on Baldwins Lane now stand on what was open land when I was a kid.

roxley Wood stands just behind my old school. It's a pleasant walk to Croxley Great Barn, Croxley Hall Farm and to the area where the Watercress beds used to be.

CROXLEY GREAT BARN

Just across the road from All Saints' church and running alongside the grounds of Rickmansworth School there is an unmade road called Lavrock Lane (Lavrock is an old name for Lark). It leads to the woods, Croxley Hall Farm and Croxley Great Barn. David and I spent a pleasant hour strolling off into the woods and taking some photographs until David discovered a railway bridge over the Metropolitan Line. The camera came out again and as we waited for a train it gave me the chance to tell David about the Great Barn.

The Great Barn is one of the oldest buildings in Croxley. It is situated on the site of Croxley Hall Farm which belongs to the Sansom family and, although it has sometimes been called a Tithe Barn, it is not. It was also known as 'Wolsey's slaughterhouse' because, in Henry VIII's time it is said to have supplied the necessary food for the Cardinal's huge feasts that were held at nearby Moor Park. It was built between 1396 and 1401 and is one of the largest barns in the county of Hertfordshire. Unfortunately, the Barn is on private land but it can be viewed by appointment.

Close by is Croxley Hall Farm which dates back to the 16th century. It is where William Sansom adopted modern techniques in watercress growing at around about the same time that John Dickinson was revolutionising the papermaking industry. Cress needs a mild climate and a good quantity of pure water and chalk streams with a controlled flow though gravel beds. The River Chess which runs through the hilly countryside of Hertfordshire and Buckinghamshire provides just these conditions. By 1820 Herts watercress was on sale in London markets and Charles Sansom of Croxley Hall Farm became a leading national authority on watercress.

We also know that watercress baskets were made in the Great Barn from osiers grown locally in the 20th century.

Croxley Great Barn

Croxley Hall Farm

THE ANNUAL GARDEN COMPETITION

In July 2006 David Thrower and I were invited to join the judges for the finals of the Annual Garden Competition. There were ten finalists and the sun shone on them, their gardens and the judges as we made our way to all corners of the village. David and I were also present at the final judging in the council chamber later in the afternoon. I'm pleased to say that we were not called upon to give an opinion because we would have awarded prizes to all concerned! Not only because of the quality of the entries but for the good humour and hospitality extended to us by the members of the council and the entrants, altogether a most pleasant exercise and insight into village life.

Our thanks and congratulations to:
Mr. and Mrs. Martin of Harvey Road, Mrs. Hargrave of Bateman Road, Mr. I. Bradley of Valley Walk, Mrs. K. Sheriff also of Bradley Walk, Mrs. D. Gander of Sycamore Road, Mr. B. Jeffreys also of Sycamore Road, Mrs. and Mr. McLachlan of Kenilworth Drive, Miss A. Mackrow Harvey of Baldwins Lane, Mr. D. Jeffs of Owens Way and Mrs. L. New of New Road.

The Judges: Dave Cartwright, Andrew Goddard, Kath Perry, Christine Jefford, Hazel Seeley Mark Saxon, accompanied by the Clerk to the Parish Council, David Allison.

"METROLAND"

The name "Metroland" was created in 1915 by the publicity department of the Metropolitan Railway. Metroland became the title of the Railway's annual booklet which described the area the Railway served through north west London, into Middlesex, Hertfordshire and Buckinghamshire. The Railway set up a separate company to develop housing and shops along the Metropolitan line. Much of the area was extensively developed between the World Wars and created a distinctive atmosphere, and Croxley became part of that development.

By 1925 Croxley had two railway stations and these modern connections to the outside world enabled the spread of London's "Metroland" to this corner of Hertfordshire. By the 1930s local builders such as Arthur Pitkin and F.J. Simmonds who traded under the name Croxley Estates began to develop land in the area. The old estate land offered investors and builders the opportunity to construct street after street of new housing and so Croxley steadily grew, with new homes available for anything between five hundred and a thousand pounds. During the Second World War building ceased and the people of Croxley got on with the business of supporting the war effort. When the Pilgrim family moved to the village during the war my dad could have purchased a three bedroom, semi-detached house for the princely sum of seven hundred and fifty pounds, if he had possessed the money. After the war development began again and the village grew steadily.

Despite the fact that people moved to Croxley to escape the vagaries of wartime London, Croxley saw some action in the shape of bombs and shells falling in the area. My brothers collected shrapnel and kept it for many years. A parachute bomb caused damage to All Saints' church and a bomb fell close to the Metropolitan station, both of these incidents brought about the destruction of properties. Common Moor, Lincoln Way and other streets also suffered.

The following photographs show many of the changes, alterations, extensions that the properties have undergone over the years. However there is still ample evidence of Metroland in Croxley Green.

In the 1940s and 1950s when I was growing up Croxley appeared to have several distinctive areas. The land around Richmond Way was still being developed and was bounded roughly by Rousebarn Lane, Little Green Lane and The Green. At the top of Baldwins Lane there were the prefabs and there was (and still is) a footpath leading from Baldwins Lane past St Oswald's church. The local policeman whose name I think was Mr. McIntosh was a man to be feared and woebetide any small boy who was caught cycling along that footpath! Perhaps Mr. McIntosh really didn't have anything better to do. In Richmond Way we played cricket and football in the middle of the road when we couldn't be bothered to go to the fields. Visiting the road now I can't believe how small it is. Baldwins Lane is almost the religious centre of Croxley. There is the Baptist church where I once read the lesson, the Methodist church where I also once read the lesson and the Catholic church where I never read the lesson (but would have done if asked). Just off Baldwins Lane is St Oswald's where I didn't read the lesson but did attend a pre school group. From this information the reader will probably glean that my mum didn't care how I got religion as long as I got it! These days the churches communicate with one another on a much broader basis and that is really good.

In fields at the bottom of Baldwins Lane women worked at rag picking for the mill in the early 20th century and straw plaiting was also prevalent in the area, Croxley being well known for its high quality straw.

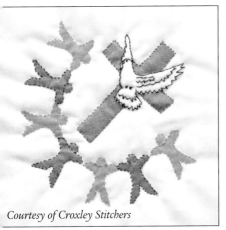

Courtesy of Croxley Stitchers

The Church Of All Saints has a special place in the Pilgrim family history because my sister June married Joe O'Mahoney there. The church is not that old considering the history of the area. I guess that, before All Saints was built, people used the church in Rickmansworth.

On the 17th of October 1869 a meeting took place to agree the building of a Chapel of Ease at Croxley Green and to ask the Master and Fellows of Gonville and Caius College, Cambridge, the Lords of the Manor for a suitable site. Many meetings followed and eventually it was agreed to build a church at the south end of the green. The Church Commissioners paid the sum of £600 for a triangular piece of land, "so shaped by the turnpike road from Watford to Rickmansworth and the road to Sarratt". Plans of the church with seating for 260 were prepared by Mr. Norton of London. They were approved and the contract for the building was given to Mr. Samuel Clarke of Bath for the sum of £2,318 3s 0d.

The district (parish) assigned to the church, considered to have a population of 1,000, was described as being bounded to the west by a line drawn along the top of Scots Hill extending towards Chandlers Cross, then to the River Gad (Gade), following the same stream to the Lock at Cassio and back.

The foundation stone of the church was laid by the Right Hon. Lord Ebury at 4 pm on September 27th, 1870. For the ceremony a temporary staging was provided and decorated with evergreens.

Church interior

Church exterior

For 34 years this building served the village well but with the growth of John Dickinson's paper mill, the local population increased and the church became very crowded and uncomfortable. On 13th September 1906, the vicar and churchwardens called for a meeting which took place on 20th September to discuss plans for enlarging the church. Mr.Temple-Moor, an architect from London, was asked if he would produce a design. Life in the parish carried on through the First World War and the list of those who had fallen began to grow. The War finally ended in November 1918. The life of the church continued through the years of depression, the General Strike, the Abdication, Coronation of George VI until World War Two. Then on 25th September 1940 at 9.35pm the East end of the church was severely damaged by a parachute mine; the tower, roof, organ, pulpit and the Lady Chapel all suffered serious damage. The damage was estimated at £13,000 excluding that done to the organ and boiler.

St Oswald's church stands in Malvern Way and, as has already been explained, was indeed my first seat of learning.

In the early 1930s as land was being developed between Baldwins Lane and Little Green Lane, it became clear that a daughter church to All Saints was required and land was acquired in 1936 in Malvern Way for the sum of £450. Confirmation from the Bishop of St Albans was obtained for the construction of a dual purpose Church Hall. As building began local residents were invited to pay one shilling for the privilege of laying a brick in the new building. It is said that, because women didn't wear trousers in those days, they laid their bricks on a lower level to the men! I am also reliably informed that cracks which appeared where the ladies had laid their bricks had nothing to do with their lack of bricklaying talents.

There was some controversy about calling the building St Oswald's but the Rev. Percy Langdon of All Saints Church explained his suggestion thus. St Oswald was born about 604 and killed at the Battle of Maserfield in 642. He was a King of Northumbria. He defeated Cadwallon at Heavenfield in 635 and established Christianity. Oswald raised the first cross over the Christian altar in Bernicia. As the Diocese is named after Alban, the first saint martyred in this country, so its latest Church Hall is named after the first king in this country who really died in defence of the Christian faith. You've got to agree that there is a kind of logic in the good Reverend's reasoning!

St Oswald's Hall is a very well used amenity and several groups and clubs meet there.

In 1940 many children were evacuated from London to Croxley and this served to swell the congregation. During the war years St Oswald's was very much the centre of the community and was in use seven days a week for various activities. For many years a shuttlecock rested in the rafters from the days when the Badminton club used the hall! While their menfolk were away at war the ladies in the congregation formed a Working Party and got busy sewing, knitting and making toys, they even knitted socks for Watford Football Club. As the war was drawing to a close the Rev. Wilkinson became the first Priest in Charge he is remembered very affectionately to this day. Wilkinson formed a Gilbert and Sullivan Society and encouraged the young people of Croxley to join him. They performed The Gondoliers at Watford Town Hall before an audience of 4,000 people! The reverend gentleman was also one of the founding members of Croxley Wanderers Football Club.

The Baptist church stands in Baldwins Lane and began its life as a temporary church in the 1940s. The present church was built in 1952 and it opened in 1953. As I have already explained, I once read the lesson there having been coached by Mr. George who lived at the top of Richmond Way. Mr. George was a very pleasant fellow and I was pleased to meet up again with his daughter Christine during the present Queen's Jubilee celebrations.

"Here comes the Boys Brigade

A tuppeny ha'penny pillbox

And half a yard of braid".

(The above courtesy of my mum, Ivy Dorothy Pilgrim)

THE BOYS' BRIGADE

William Smith was born on 27th October 1854 at Pennyland House, Thurso, Scotland. At the age of 15 years he moved to Glasgow to work in his uncle's business. While there, he joined the Volunteers and by the time he was 19 he had become a Lance Corporal in the 1st Lanarkshire Rifle Volunteers. The very same year he joined the church after hearing the evangelists Moody & Sankey.

By 1883 William Smith had become a Lieutenant and was teaching in the North Woodside Mission Sunday School. The boys in his Sunday school class were a challenge, and he was open to new ideas about how best to deal with them. Someone suggested that the methods used in the Volunteers might be appropriate, and by this inspiration the Boys' Brigade was created. William Smith took a leading role in the new organisation, accepting a full-time post as the first Brigade Secretary in 1887. He worked non-stop for the movement, on two occasions even crossing the Atlantic to promote the Boys' Brigade in Canada and the U.S.A. Throughout, he remained Captain of the 1st Glasgow company, rarely missing a meeting. William Smith died on 10th May 1914 after being suddenly taken ill at a Boys' Brigade meeting in London. Smith was knighted by King Edward VII for his services to boys.

The Boys' Brigade was attached to the church and, for a short while, I became involved. I have to admit that the Boys' Brigade first attracted me because it had a football team which played its games on a pitch at the top of Baldwins Lane in Croxley. A neighbour of ours was a member and he encouraged me to join. My mum duly purchased a hat and a couple of other accoutrements for me and I was accepted into the Brigade. My first match was a disaster as was my first parade. Our neighbour chastised me for wearing poorly ironed trousers and I (being a rather proud person who considered his remarks as a slur on my dear old mum) took exception. I told him what he could do with his brigade. In truth my anger was due to a poor performance in the soccer team where I gave away a penalty. So I left the Brigade but continued to visit the church.

The church runs an array of community orientated activities including the Sparkling All Stars, Pulse, Trail Blazers, Axis Youth Group, Good Companions, Young Mums' Bible Study and of course, the good old Boys' Brigade.

The Christian Fellowship has been in Croxley Green since 1892 and people regularly met in a house near the windmill. A Gospel Hall was purchased at the top of Scots Hill but this was destroyed by enemy action in the Second World War. The Dickinson Guild House was used for some years for Sunday meetings until a site was acquired in Fuller Way where a corrugated iron building was erected and used until a new building was opened in 1959. The Fellowship is a Bible based church, believing that the Bible is the inspired word of God.

In 1866, a Methodist by the name of Pierce came to Croxley Green and, finding no Methodist chapel, established a Methodist Society in his own house. Within 18 months, on 16th February 1868, the first Methodist chapel was opened in New Road on a plot of land costing £25. By 1892 the increased population of Croxley Green meant that a new chapel and schoolroom were needed. The schoolroom was completed in November 1892, and was then used for worship whilst the new chapel was built. Events moved on apace, as the new chapel was ready and opened on 30th April 1893. The whole project cost £1,087! Further developments included the installation of a pipe organ in 1947 to replace the harmonium, and the construction of the new hall at the rear of the premises in the late 1960s. Today the premises consist of the main church, a large hall and a newly refurbished kitchen, toilet and a disabled toilet. There are some halls attached to the church where all kind of activities take place including parent and toddler clubs, fellowship groups and the Girls Brigade.

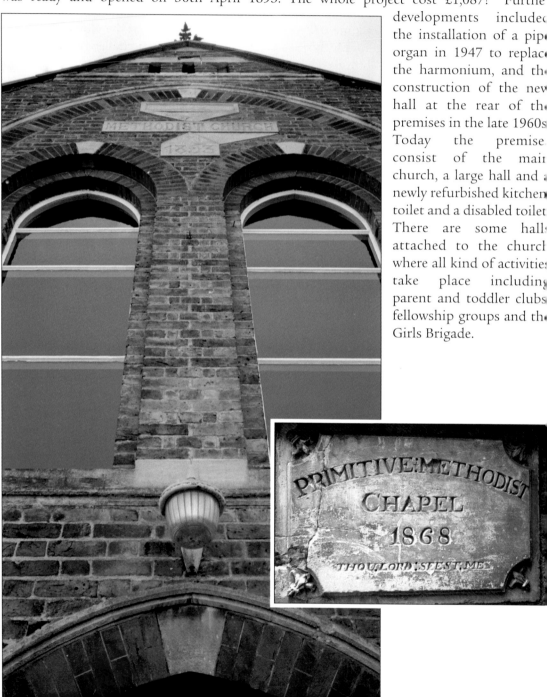

88

The first Roman Catholic services in Croxley were held in the British Restaurant on Winton Drive during the Second World War. In 1938 Cardinal Hinsley gave Father Evariste Buytaers (what a wonderful name), the newly appointed Parish Priest of Rickmansworth the responsibility for providing a Chapel of Ease in Croxley and in 1939 a site in Baldwins Lane was purchased for £450 and tenders were received for the building to be constructed on the site but in September of that year the Cardinal ordered that all building on churches and schools should cease on the outbreak of war. In 1940 the Rector looked for a Mass Centre and Durrants Hall was used on Sunday mornings until 1942. Dickinson's Hall and the British Restaurant were also used. In 1942 the Baldwins Lane site was requisitioned for allotments and it was not until 1951 that construction of a church on Baldwins Lane finally began. In 1958 St Teresa's Chapel of Ease became the Parish of St Bede.

THE RAILWAY STATIONS

Very little of Croxley Green 'LMS' station still exists and it did have a somewhat difficult beginning as well. The station opened in 1912 and linked Croxley with Watford, and in the 1950s it was the line that allowed me to visit my grandma in London. I would never have dreamt of allowing my children to travel alone when they were young but things were different when I was growing up and I thought nothing of changing trains three times to get to Chiswick where Grandma 'Daisy' Stanton would be sitting in her front room ready to offer me Heinz Tomato Soup laced with peas and spuds!

It was really rather sad to see the state of the station now and as for the difficult beginning the Herts Advertiser of 15th March 1913 contained an article about a "Supposed Outrage by Suffragettes". It seems that in the early hours of the 11th of March the local policeman, PC Wilcox, said good evening to two ladies walking close to the station and soon after noticed smell of burning. On investigation the worthy 'copper' saw that the station was on fire. The article continues: "No Sunday trains run upon the loop, and the station is closed from about 10 o'clock on Saturday night to 6.30 on Monday. Last Saturday night the premises were locked up and everything left in the usual way. About 1.40 on Monday morning PC Wilcox was on his beat, which extended to the bridge near the stream. He became aware of a smell of burning. The odour increased as he approached the bridge, and when he came in view of the station he saw flames rising from the centre of the platform. As soon as the fire was extinguished, a break down gang started to clear the line of debris, and later in the day carpenters commenced the erection of a temporary platform on the other side of the line".

"The general opinion of those who are acquainted with the locality and the way in which the fire broke out is that it must have been caused by Suffragettes, but there are no clues to directly place the responsibility on them. Two women, strangers to the locality, were seen walking along Scots Hill towards Rickmansworth about an hour and half before the fire was discovered, and on Tuesday morning the officials at Croxley Green Station received through the post a copy of the publication called "The Suffragette". Written on the wrappers were the words "Afraid copy left got burnt". These circumstances establish no direct connection between the Suffragettes and the fire, whether they are worth taking into account as factors supporting the conclusion that the Suffragettes were the culprits is another matter". Apart from the observation that the article is overly long and that I was always taught not to place a comma before the word 'and', I think that the journalist missed a vital clue. The link with the Suffragettes is the fact that when the station was built they only put in a 'Gents' loo. Now if that wasn't sufficient provocation for a bunch of feisty ladies, I don't know what is!

NB Despite having been closed for some time the station reopened on 4th December 1982, to take football fans to Vicarage Road on Saturdays to see the 'Hornets' play home games. By the 1990s this facility had ceased.

Croxley Metropolitan Station opened in 1925, presumably to serve the fast growing population in the area. Our annual summer visit to the seaside began at this station. Mum, Dad, my two sisters and I would walk from Richmond Way lugging our suitcases and bursting with excitement. It must have been an exhausting journey for Mum and Dad, who would travel to London, hop on an Underground train and then catch the steam train to Clacton on Sea. It is a sign of the times that one can see taxis waiting for customers outside the station these days. Oh, what Mum and Dad would have given for a cab!

I insisted that David Thrower included a photograph of the boundary fence at the station, which runs along the Watford Road, because my brother George and I once painted it by hand during the winter! I have measured it and cannot believe that we even contemplated the task. We must have needed the money badly because David reckons that it is at least a quarter of a mile long, but he does tend to exaggerate. Take a look at it and ask yourself, would you want to paint that by hand? George cannot recall who gave him the job, which is just as well because I still want a word with that person. I want to ask him if anyone else has been called upon since to be subjected to freezing hands and a worn out paint brush.

For me New Road conjures up memories of Jackson the butcher, the lovely Freda who took the money while Henry wrapped the meat, the 'trades' bike my brother rode when delivering meat, Dickinson's Guild House where we paid the council rates and a small shop close to the Red House where we purchased confectionary such as sherbet dabs, sticks of barley sugar and Refreshers! Jackson's had sawdust on the floor, strings of sausages hanging in the window and dripping. Toast covered in meat dripping was the standard weekday breakfast in our house, egg and bacon was for Sundays. New Road was originally a footpath between the Red House and the Artichoke on the Green, then it became Croxley New Road and finally just New Road.

Shops first appeared in New Road at the turn of the 19th century and there were other businesses as well, including a wheelwright and a blacksmith. Later Mr. Stone (he of Stone's Cherry Orchard) ran his coal delivery business from New Road.

'THE GUILD HOUSE'

Its proper name was the Dickinson Institute and when it opened in December 1895, there was a reading room and a social club founded by the manager of Dickinson's Mill, Mr Charles Barton Smith. The original address was 32 Milestone Field, later Dickinson Square. Another, larger building was opened one year later and spectators were treated to a firework display accompanied by music. In 1928 the place became known as the House of Dickinson so don't ask me why we all called it the Guild House although there is evidence it was renamed the House of Dickinson Guild so I might have been right after all. During World War One it was used as a convalescent home for servicemen. Notwithstanding the different names, the building sadly burned down in 1966. A traditional ceremony was carried out on May 1st each year. The little girls of the village would go from house to house with gaily decorated hoops singing a song.

"The Garland, the Garland,
A very pretty garland,
As ever you wish to see,
It's fit for Queen Victori-ar
So please remember me"

After the death of Queen Victoria, the fourth line was changed to

"It's fit for Queen Alexandri-ar".

Courtesy of Croxley Stitchers

Barton Way? Well Maybe

A good number of residents of Croxley Green will be aware that Barton Way is named after Charles Barton-Smith who was manager at Dickinson's Mill for some years. What they might not know is that there is just a chance that the road was misnamed!

Before Charles was born his family were living in Gravesend, his father was just plain Thomas Smith who worked as a Customs Officer. By 1861 Thomas Smith and his family had moved to Mile End Road in London. Charles was born in Gravesend and was six years old when the family name (still plain Smith) shows up on the census for London. In 1871 the Smiths were living at 9 Clinton Road, Mile End Old Town, Mr. Smith was working as an 'Examining Officer for HM Customs' and young Charles, now sixteen, was employed as a stationer's clerk. Ten years later Charles Smith appears at 78 Clinton Road, he is married to Mary Louise and they have one son also named Charles. By 1891 Charles has added a 'B' between the Charles and the Smith. He is employed as a Papermaker's Manager and he and his wife have six children, so perhaps the 'B' stood for 'busy'.

By 1901 Charles is in Croxley Green at 'Lindiswara' and is now calling himself Charles Barton-Smith. Now it may be that Barton was a baptismal name and that Charles only used it when he began climbing the ladder of success. Whether it was or wasn't his real name doesn't really matter because he certainly did well for himself, his family and for the people of Croxley Green and anyway, Smith Way wouldn't really have worked!

Barton-Smith stood for the Rickmansworth Urban District Council in 1898 and won three hundred and eighty three votes, the highest number of any of the other candidates. He became Chairman of the council in 1904.

The Barton-Smith children didn't have to work in the way their father and his brothers and sisters had. At 'Lindiswara' there were two servants, Emma Hester, the cook and Ada Child the housemaid. Charles died in 1929.

Towards the top end of New Road and close to the Green there is a small close named after Madame Tussaud, the lady who founded the famous waxworks. She was born in Strasbourg in 1761, as Marie Grosholtz. She modelled the author Voltaire in 1777 and became art tutor to King Louis XVI's sister in 1780. During this period of her life Marie was with the French court at Versailles, but returned to Paris in 1789. After the French Revolution of 1789, she was imprisoned in LaForce prison with aristocrats and others associated with the regime. Here she shared a cell with the future Empress Josephine (Napoleon Bonaparte's wife). On her release in 1794 Marie married Francois Tussaud. She took her collection of wax masks of guillotined aristocrats and relics of the French revolution on a tour of Britain in 1802. In 1835, she established a base for the collection at the Baker Street Bazaar in London. In 1846 it was the famous Punch magazine that coined the phrase 'Chamber of Horrors'. Madame Tussaud died in 1850. John Theodore Tussaud, great grandson of Marie, lived at the Hawthorns in New Road. Theodore began to study modelling and sculpture under his father and, when his father retired he succeeded him as artist to the exhibition. The 1949 Kelly's Directory also shows an A. R. Tussaud living at number 48 Copthorne Road.

THE SCHOOLS

Alittle over a hundred years ago a few of the village children could secure some education from one of two sources: Granny Blackwell's dame school at Smokeys, which was on Scots Hill, or they could go to a plaiting school at Elias Stranger's on the Green where they would learn to read and write as well as straw plaiting. Thankfully Croxley Green has some rather more enlightened establishments these days.

Courtesy of Croxley Stitchers

The first school in Croxley was built in 1873 on land donated by John Dickinson in Garden Road. It opened in 1875 and 120 attended. Garden Road was renamed Yorke Road in 1898 in honour of Charles Yorke who had been chairman of Rickmansworth Urban District Council. By 1894 the village school had 296 pupils and the boys moved to the new school in Watford Road. The school continued to grow and by 1938 570 children were crammed into the classrooms. Then fire partly destroyed some of the building and the managers handed over the schools to Hertfordshire County Council.

DURRANTS SCHOOL

My sister June and my brothers Bill and George attended Durrants. My brothers' attendance was somewhat more sporadic than June's because, a) June was prone to do what she was told and, b) Bill and George had other more interesting things to occupy their minds.

BROTHER BILL REMEMBERS DURRANTS SCHOOL

"My early school years were spent at Harvey Road School and then Durrants School in the early '40s.

"My first memories of the teaching staff at the school conjure up visions of the redoubtable Miss Slight (ugh) and the young gyrating gym mistress Miss Short (whew). Miss Short's prowess on the hockey field stirred many a young girl's heart and mind, as did her movements on and off the field for young boys whose sap was just beginning to rise. Miss Slight who 'took geography' was a different kettle of fish. A much older and grim faced lady, she had a no nonsense-approach to teaching. For example when a pupil dared to put up a hand and say, 'Please Miss, I haven't got a pencil', she would reply, 'You stupid child, get on with your work', then at the end of the lesson she would question, 'Why haven't you done your work?' 'Please Miss, I didn't have a pencil.' Miss Slight snorted, 'You stupid child' and dished out fifty lines. She was probably a nice lady outside school." Just as a footnote to this story you might like to know that brother George claims that it happened to him and not Bill but squabbling between brothers is unseemly so we will move on.

BILL SAYS

"Mr. Durrell my carpentry teacher, whose dribbling lips moved curiously in unison with the motion of his tenon saw, wearied of my efforts to construct even one half of a bookend. Although I tried very hard to gain his approval I was unable to finish off even the simplest task, but he recognised my efforts and rewarded me at an end of term exam by providing the missing bookend. What a gent!

"Mr. Stone was an elderly man, gruff in manner and a strict disciplinarian. He was short in stature, grey haired and had a gammy leg. Fortunately I didn't come across him often but one day he grabbed me by the scruff of my neck, drawing blood, for allegedly running in the corridor. I remember the sting of his long dirty fingernails still. My favourite master was Mr. Stiles. He took several classes including sports and football in particular. I realised much later that 'Stilesy' was coaxing me to play but I didn't have any boots so he loaned me a pair that I had to stuff with newspaper to make them fit. Come the day I was rushing around the field flinging all of my considerable self at anyone who was wearing the wrong coloured shorts when I found myself near the goalmouth. Someone shouted, 'Shoot', and I lashed out at the ball with my left foot, which was the wrong one as I'm right footed and scored. After the match 'Stilesy' said 'You played a blinder Pilgo', and I blushed happily but as I removed my boots I found I'd put them on the wrong feet!"

BROTHER GEORGE

If Bill was a somewhat eccentric footballer brother George was certainly much more mainstream. George was a very early member of the Croxley Wanderers and a stalwart in the Durrants school side, he played for Watford Boys and also represented the County in athletics. At the age of seventeen George disappeared off to Australia carrying just a small bag containing his possessions. Five years later he returned to Croxley Green in a black London cab, which he had booked on disembarking from the boat at Harwich. To my young mind the mere idea of hiring a cab was enough, let alone riding in one from Harwich to Croxley Green! Come to think of it, I wouldn't even contemplate it now.

George is second from the left in the back row. How many of the other players can you name?

The area where Durrants once stood is now a housing development. The school finally closed in 1991 having ensured that many a local lad and lass began life with a good education.

Sister June Remembers

"When war was declared I was nearly ten years old and I was evacuated to Weymouth but my stay did not last long because Dad was asked to re-locate to Croxley Green and became caretaker of 'The Grove' for H.J. Heinz and Company. Once my family had settled into the house in Richmond Way I joined them. I started school at Durrants Secondary Modern along with brothers George and Bill. Sometimes we were sent potato picking in Farmer Foster's field. One day we were called into the school hall and given bars of Cadbury's chocolate which I think had been sent from Rhodesia! The school allowed me to have a week off to help my mother when my brother John was born in 1942.

"I recall the air raid siren going off one day and Mum and me trying to find Bill and George who had 'bunked off' school to play in the woods. I was allowed to leave school at the age of fourteen and got a job at Jay's furniture stores in Watford. Mum worked at Croxley Mill for a while. There were air raid shelters at The Grove and we used to sleep there when Dad was on fire duty. We used to go to the dances at the Guild House in Croxley and that is where I met my future husband Joe, his grandparents ran the Coach and Horses on the Green."

More Memories from Bill

"The classes at Durrants School were grouped in 'houses', Norman, Saxon, Celt and Dane, each being identified by a coloured sash during competitive sports. The 'houses' also competed with each other to collect salvage for the war effort and as iron railings and gates of houses were torn down to be converted into precious metal so bands of schoolchildren scavenged far and wide for paper, cardboard and metal objects to be weighed at school to accrue points for their house.

"I was one of a trio of Normans who poked around the groundsman's shed on the local golf course and gathered bits and pieces of scrap that I now know to have been rather important parts of grounds maintenance equipment! We loaded this 'scrap' on to a home-made trolley and made haste to the school flushed with success. Doubtless the groundsman was more than a bit flushed the next day when he discovered the loss.

"Despite a lengthy interrogation at the weigh-in our contribution set the scales soaring and the Normans were awarded record points.

"It was on the same golf course where my close friend Johnny and I climbed a stunted, dying oak tree and for some illogical reason lit a small fire of twigs in a cavity in the trunk. The fire started brightly enough then smouldered and, despite our best efforts, simply would not go out. We conferred hastily and agreed not to call the fire brigade but that I would find water to extinguish the blaze. I raced off down the hill and along Rousebarn Lane all the way home to Richmond Way to fill a lemonade bottle from the tap and return puffing and panting to find that Johnny had decided upon a more natural method to deal with the emergency. He was just buttoning his fly as I flopped exhausted on the ground. 'Johnny' was Johnny Bastable, who lived in Links Way. He matured into a great banjo player, playing with the renowned Ken Collyer band for many years and later formed his own traditional jazz band, the Chosen Six. Sadly Johnny passed away a few years ago."

Mum with George, Bill and June, The Grove Croxley Green 1940

LITTLE GREEN LANE SCHOOL

I am grateful to the present Headteacher, Graham Metcalfe, for the following brief history of a school which was responsible for my entry to the hallowed halls of Rickmansworth Grammar School via the eleven plus exam. Built to meet the post-war need for hundreds of new schools, Little Green School was opened on Monday, 6th May 1949. Designed by Hertfordshire County Architect, David Medd, the school was built on its five acre site to reflect architectural qualities of space, light, colour and geometrical order. It even features in a book – *'Great Architecture of the World'*.

"The school is like a pavilion in a park", said Charles Wymer, a schoolboy at Little Green when it first opened. All the classrooms in the main building face south across the playing fields, which are ringed with trees.

William Worthy was Headteacher from 1949 until 1959. Ron Watson, who retired in 1984, succeeded him. Mrs. Judith Exley was Headteacher from 1984 until 1988; Alex Miller succeeded her and was in post from 1989 until 1997. The present Headteacher has been in post since January 1998.

Quite apart from the fact that young Charles Wymer displayed a wonderful knowledge of the English language, I would like to thank the present Head for the information that Mr. Worthy's Christian name was 'William'! I guess that these days all the kids know teacher's first names but it would not have been quite the thing when I was seven years old. It was William Worthy's wife who my mother thanked for seeing me into Ricky Grammar. Mrs Worthy was, as I recall, a lady not to be trifled with; not someone to fear, just not to be trifled with. I have already explained that attending school was not high on my agenda but Mrs.

Worthy persevered with me long after her colleagues had given up the challenge and I am grateful for that now even if I wasn't at the time. We kids didn't really look upon teachers as being ordinary members of the human race or indeed as people who had private lives. Looking back, I guess that Mrs. Worthy was a pretty normal person, she must have been because, one afternoon, when she had finished reading a chapter from *Tom Sawyer* to us, she asked Dudley Withers and myself what we were giggling about. I informed her that we were discussing the book she had been reading from and she asked which particular piece. I said "The bit about spunky water" and she just gave a knowing nod and a brief smile – I mean, you wouldn't have thought that a teacher would know about 'spunk', would you? But I admit that the lady went up in my estimation.

I haven't been able to find the photograph of the school band which was taken on the occasion of our appearance at Watford Town Hall which is a shame because standing in the back row is an angelic Pilgrim sporting a check shirt, black silky type shorts and a bow tie! And holding the only musical instrument he has ever been capable of playing – a triangle. It is probably best for you not to have seen that picture but here are some others of Little Green JMI.

Picture the scene, it is circa 1949 and a 'crocodile' of small boys and girls, in twos and holding hands are making their way to their brand new school. There is much excited chatter, because although these kids are already attending school it is not a 'proper' school. Prior to moving to Malvern Way I attended two makeshift places of learning. St' Oswald's Church Hall and a Scout Hut! When Malvern Way opened its doors on the 6th of May 1949, it had real classrooms, blackboards, a playground and plenty of open fields and it also had a school nurse, for goodness sake. Mention Malvern Way School to me even now and that school nurse comes immediately to mind, not because I have fantasies of people in nurse's uniforms (but there again I might) but because I had warts. It may well have been standard practice at the time but to me it was barbaric. The nurse scraped away the best part of my three warts and then soaked my hand in iodine. I'm pretty sure they don't do that these days. I am equally sure that Malvern Way School is set in wonderful surroundings complete with a pond area, a spinney and an area of historic woodland.

Rickmansworth School

I have already related how I came to be a somewhat reluctant pupil at what was then Rickmansworth Grammar School so we won't go over that again. Sufficient to say that the school was part of the brave new world where girls and boys would be taught together and that most of us were grateful for that. In the very early days the builders were still working on the school and we took great delight in removing the putty from the windows, much to the annoyance of the construction gang.

Mr. Kenyon ruled the sports department and frightened the life out of us and many years later I met him at a reunion and couldn't understand how I could have been so scared of such a little man. Because this was a brand new school in a brave new educational era, the Headmaster was determined that we should understand just how lucky we were and also to establish the school as a force to be reckoned with in the area. Mr. Kenyon was at the vanguard of the Head's drive and he duly drove us on the rugby and cricket fields until we dropped. In our first couple of years our rugby team 'stuffed' Watford Grammar School on their home pitch and Letchworth, Hitchin and even Old Merchant Taylors succumbed. Mr. Heddle (history) helped out on the cricket field and we did pretty well at the summer game as well. As training we picked stones from our fledgling pitches and played our home games at Old Merchant Taylors' Durrants pitch.

Rickmansworth Grammar School staff photograph

Apart from falling in love with two or three comely wenches and trying desperately to obtain 'dates' with them, I couldn't really see what the school had to offer me and so I was content to leave. Little did I know exactly how much knowledge those devious teachers had managed to impart. Over the years I have become profoundly grateful for their hard work. Mr. Withers who I did not like, managed to instil in me the ability to discover classical music in my later life. At the time all I was interested in was the size of his adam's apple as it wobbled away whilst he was singing Handel's Messiah, later in life I realised that it was well worth a listen.

Rickmansworth Grammar School Rugby Team circa 1954 including an angelic looking future author, front row second from the right!

Jan Field, formerly Watton contacted me after a gap of about thirty years, when she saw one of my books in a shop and remembered my name from our days at Ricky Grammar. Jan lives in Norfolk now but became involved with the former pupils of our school through their magazine, the Rosarian. So involved that she masterminded a tapestry for the school's Jubilee

couldn't help myself! I simply had to obtain Jan's permission to include some of her schoolday memories, which are particularly on the subject of the school uniform.

JAN SAYS

School tie was maroon and girls' knickers were grey, dark green blazers and cardigans, light green shirts and grey socks (winter uniform). As skirts were becoming shorter and shorter, Millie Collings (Headmistress) used to call in anyone suspected of raising the hemlines too far after assembly (when her eagle eye would identify them) for a 'kneeling session'. If the skirt did not touch the floor in the kneeling position it was 'get it right for tomorrow or stay at home and I will talk with your parents' time."

Jan attended St Joan of Arc School prior to going to Ricky Grammar and for her there was a real surprise on her first day at the big school. "A first year at RGS came as a culture shock, from going to a school where everything possible remained covered by clothing to one where we marched past the whole school each games afternoon in our knickers because the local suppliers did not have the green Moygashel shorts. That was some year for me". I've got news for Jan, it was some year for us boys as well! As for Moygashel, Jan, who is much brighter than me because she stayed on at school, tells me that it is a type of material designed so that it does not blow up in the wind! A good reason as to why the school should have chosen this (Irish) material in the first place but it doesn't explain why the girls were allowed to be immodest for over a year.

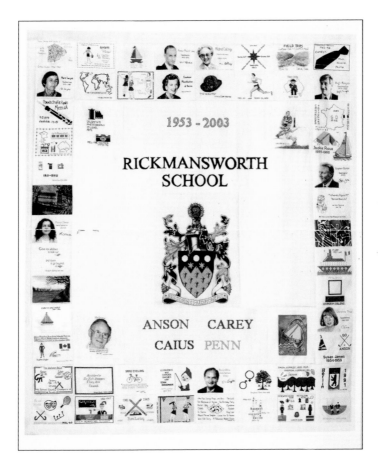

CROXLEY COMMON MOOR

The Moor was a place pretty much to be avoided when I was a kid. There was a character named 'Albert Sarratt' who lived there with his mum, or so it was said. My only real memory of 'Albert' was a rather frightening chap who talked to himself so perhaps, in another life, he had been a schoolteacher! My friend Ralph Hitchcock recalls a character named 'Pigeon East' who had much the same characteristics so maybe they were one and the same man. Ralph told me that the gentleman used to stuff the tyres of his bike with grass!

Much of the land surrounding the Moor has been built on or improved for modern agriculture but Common Moor itself is relatively unchanged. Its 100 acres of historic grassland straddle the flood plain of the River Gade. It is the action of the river scouring across the plain, combined with centuries of grazing which have produced the rich and diverse plant life that we see today. Due to this ancient connection between grazing animal and the wildlife, continued grazing is essential to the protection of Common Moor. Without their appetite the site would soon become covered in dense scrub and coarse grasses, leaving no room for the wide variety of flowering plants currently found.

The Moor has been registered as a Site of Special Scientific Interest due to the rarity of its plant life and is also a designated Local Nature Reserve in acknowledgement of the contribution local residents make to its management. This protection is essential because there are only one or two similar valley sites in existence in Hertfordshire.

Croxley Common Moor is to be found to the south east of Croxley Green, a short distance from the Underground station. It is also accessible from the Grand Union Canal towpath and the Ebury Way. The site can be freely explored, however please note that there are no surfaced paths and some areas become boggy, especially in winter. Over 130 different types of plant have been noted on the Moor and there are probably many more. The small scale changes in the lie of the land dramatically increase the diversity. Even the old anthills are tall enough to affect the plant species found on them.

Where the ground is raised, the freely draining sandy soils and gravels produce exceptionally dry ground, poor in nutrients and favouring plants such as harebell, yarrow, devil's bit scabious, self-heal, whin, dyer's greenweed, meadow buttercup, knapweed and heather. Marshland can be found generally towards the western end of the site, or where the ground falls into hollows due to minor gravel working or the ancient course of the river. Here the soil becomes waterlogged, leading to an altogether different collection of plants like yellow iris, purple loosestrife, meadowsweet, cuckoo flower, ragged robin and marsh marigold.

The free-flowing, clear waters of the River Gade provide a home to an abundance of plant and animal life. Look out for numerous fish darting between the submerged reeds. Plants such as the water crowfoot, unbranched bur-reed, water mint and arrowhead can also be found here.

Dotted across the Moor are hundreds of small humps. These are the workings of the yellow meadow ant and have taken many decades to develop into the network you see. The ants make a tasty meal for green woodpeckers and even if you don't see a woodpecker you are likely to hear the call of these beautiful birds: listen out for their mocking laugh or 'yaffle'.

It would be impossible to include all of the games, hobbies and pastimes that exist or once did exist in Croxley Green so my apologies if I have missed out your favourite, perhaps you should have returned my call!

CROXLEY NEEDLECRAFTERS

You wil have noticed throughout this book David Throwers photographs of some of the fantastic work carried out by Croxley Needlecrafters. We are grateful to them for allowing us to reproduce their work which will form The Croxley Quilt.

The 'stitch club' was formed in 1998 with the aim of bringing together local needleworkers. The meetings are very informal and offer a chance to enjoy your hobby with other like minded people as well as the opportunity for a good old natter, a cup of tea and some chocolate biscuits!

Occasional workshops to expand the stitchers' knowledge of various types of needlework are held. In the past these workshops have included shadow appliqué, Japanese braiding, blackwork embroidery, Hardanger embroidery and drawn thread work.

Since 2001 the group have been working on a wallhanging as a group project. It consists of panels featuring aspects of Croxley Green such as the schools and clubs, the pubs, the historic houses, fauna and flora. Many of the designs are original having been charted by club members. Local artist John Kirkham has helped them to get the project up and running.

For further details visit the website www.croxleyneedlecrafters.co.uk

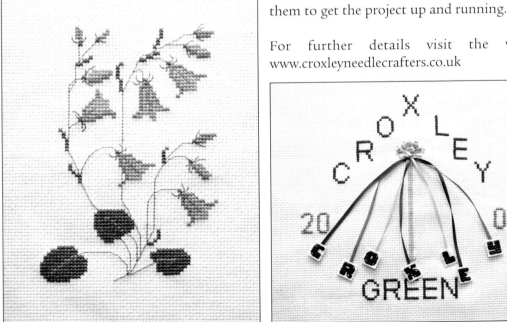

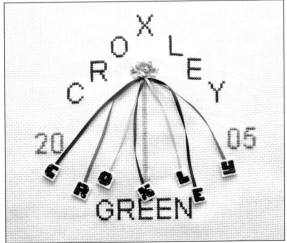

CROXLEY WANDERERS

The Youth Fellowship was established in Croxley Green by the Reverend Ray Wilkinson in the early 1940s and from that the seeds of the idea to form a football club grew. The idea came from Bill Roberts in 1947 and Rev. Wilkinson gave the plan his blessing. In the early days the team played at Barton Way. Bill Roberts was soon booking coaches to take the team to away games and this meant that the youngsters got to visit such places as the Cadbury sports complex in Birmingham, when two teams travelled and were treated to a huge meal after their games. Interest in the club grew and Bill pays tribute to Mr. Taylor and Mr. Paver who came on board to assist him. Mr. Paver worked at the NAAFI and purchased the team's 'proper' shirts. Bathing facilities were installed when the team joined the Great Western Combination and food for the visitors was supplied by a café on Watford Road. Several of the lads went on to play in a higher grade of soccer among them Jim Pettit, Leon Good and young Falconer had trials with Aston Villa. Sadly Jim Puddephat died soon after joining Arsenal. My brother George went on to play for Watford Boys, as did Derek Walton.

Croxley Wanderers

In August 1960 some of the staff at Dickinson's Paper Mill who had a mutual interest in photography got together and decided to establish a Camera Club to promote the "Science and Art of Photography". This group included Geoff Hermon who is still a member today and Dick and Marie Hassel who remained members for many years. Initially there were eleven members and the Club met every two weeks in the Dickinson Guild House on the corner of New Road and Dickinson Square where the Guild House Flats stand today.

It was difficult to attract speakers and judges to the new club and meetings usually consisted of members passing on information about prints and darkroom technique. In 1964 Kath Howard came to Croxley and she became club stalwart. Kath had been a member at Watford Camera Club since 1934 and celebrated her 100th birthday in 2006. The Club survived its early years purely by the enthusiasm of its founding members and soon became known as the "Friendly Club". Membership rose to over 100 and this made the club more financially stable and members were able to purchase some items of equipment. The club became more and more successful, winning several prestigious competitions and organising regular summer outings.

In August 1972 Rickmansworth Council gave notice that the Dickinson Guild House was unsafe and had to be closed. After a couple of years meeting at the Rickmansworth Cricket, Hockey and Sports Club the members returned to Croxley Green in January 1974 when St Oswald's Church Hall became available for its weekly meetings.

Croxley Camera Club is approaching fifty years old and still meets at St Oswald's every Wednesday evening between September and April, with a varied programme of speakers and competitions catering for most types of photographic interests. Every March the Club presents their Annual Show and produces a local calendar. The Club has supported the Revels on Croxley Green for many years. New members are always welcome and further details of the Club can be obtained from the current Chairman, Paul Bradley (01923-220240).

CROXLEY GREEN GARDENING CLUB

The origins of the Croxley Green Horticultural & Allotment Holders Society date to the end of World War One, when the Allotment movement was becoming increasingly popular. In the early days the Society had several vice-presidents, largely consisting of local 'grandees' such as Colonel Rothery-Moss. They were eminent householders with large gardens and they employed gardeners. They did not pay subscriptions but donated annual sums of money (up to £25) in support of a local gardening organisation. When the Second World War ended things began to change with Vice-Presidents increasingly drawn from the active membership who did their own gardening.

DIY gardening is the basis of present day club organisation. For more information you can visit the club website at www.croxleygardenclub.org

The committee was formed in 1982 under Town and Country Planning legislation as a representative public body to formulate a Management Plan for the then newly-established Conservation Area of The Green at Croxley. The Plan was formally adopted by Three Rivers District Council in 1983. Its implementation devolved upon Croxley Green Parish Council on its formation in 1986.

CROXLEY GREEN WINE GUILD

The Croxley Guild of Winemakers was founded in 1970 when home winemaking was in its heyday and there were over six hundred clubs across the country. The first meetings were in the Sportsman on the Green and the Guild then moved to the Dickinson Hall. The members moved several times over the years and home these days is at the Red Cross Welcome Club in Barton Way. Brewing home made beer is a really viable proposition with commercial products becoming more expensive. The club welcomes new members and Secretary Muriel Hellery is the person to contact on 01923 442458.

CROXLEY GREEN BOWLS CLUB

Bowls is a game I really fancy taking up and since it is alive and well in my home town I might just join!

ALL SAINTS BADMINTON CLUB

The club has been going for about fifty years and has teams in South West Herts league and the Chalfont District league.

My thanks to Mrs Crocker for sending us this photo of a happy bunch of members.

A fine new library stands on the corner of Barton Way and New Road on the site where the original building burned down in January 1993. Without Sylvia and her colleagues, research for this book would have been much more difficult.

CROXLEY TENNIS CLUB

The tennis club headquarters are to found on the site of the Croxley Guild of Sport and there is a wonderful, typically English clubhouse.

RED CROSS CENTRE

The Red Cross Centre has been active in Croxley Green since the First World War when it was set up as a temporary hospital at Dickinson's Institute. A detachment of First Aiders was formed in 1939 but disbanded in 1946. In the 1950s Mr. G. Wilcox formed a club for the elderly. They met in his house to begin with but then moved to the Guild House. When the membership grew to fifty Mr. Wilcox asked the Red Cross to take over. The Welcome Club, as it was known, held twice weekly meetings. A new centre was opened on the present site in 1966. Many other groups use the facility. Croxley also has a British Red Cross Sunnyside Club for the Disabled.

The International Red Cross and Red Crescent Movement started over 140 years ago. It was the brainchild of the Swiss businessman Henry Dunant. He showed great concern at the suffering of thousands of men, on both sides, who were left to die due to lack of care at the Battle of Solferino in 1859. Dunant suggested the creation of national relief societies to be made up of volunteers who would be trained to provide neutral and impartial help to relieve the suffering in times of war. A committee, which later became the International Committee of the Red Cross, was established in Geneva. Henry Dunant also proposed that countries should adopt an international agreement, which would recognise the status of medical services and of the wounded on the battlefield. This agreement - the original Geneva Convention - was adopted in 1864.

THE BRITISH RED CROSS

On 4 August 1870 a public meeting was held in London and a resolution passed that "a National Society be formed in this country for aiding sick and wounded soldiers in time of war and that the said Society be formed upon the Rules laid down by the Geneva Convention of 1864". The British National Society for Aid to the Sick and Wounded in War was formed and rendered aid and relief to both warring armies during the Franco-Prussian War and in subsequent wars and campaigns during the 19th century under the protection of the red cross emblem.

CROXLEY GREEN FLOWER GROUP

Meets the second Tuesday of each month, except August, at 7.45pm at the Red Cross Centre Barton Way; they have a flower demonstration each month.

CROXLEY GREEN ENGLISH FOLK DANCE CLUB

The club evolved from an adult education class and in 1951 it registered with the English Folk Dance and Song Society.

The club meets at St Bede's Hall, Baldwins Lane, Croxley Green on Tuesdays at 8.00pm.

CROXLEY GREEN OLD TIME DANCING CLUB

The dancing club holds its meetings at the British Legion Hall, Watford Road, Croxley Green from 8.00pm - 10.30pm on Tuesdays.

CROXLEY GUILD OF SPORTS & SOCIAL CLUB

The sporting life of Croxley was well catered for by the Dickinsons Mill. Cricket, rifle shooting, football, bowls and hockey sections were among the early pastimes enjoyed by all. The club which is situated on the Green still exists as a social club.

Main entrance to the Social Club

This Memorial stands outside the main entrance to the club

Photograph of the Football Team supplied by the club

The first official Legion Poppy Day was held in Britain on 11 November 1921, inspired by the poem *In Flanders' Fields* written by John McCrae. Since then the Poppy Appeal has been a key annual event in the nation's calendar. Some of the fiercest battles of World War One took place in Flanders and Picardy in Belgium and Northern France. In the aftermath the poppy was the only flower to appear. John McCrae was a doctor serving in the area with the Canadian Armed Forces.

In Flanders' Fields

In Flanders' fields the poppies blow
Between the crosses, row on row,
That mark our place: and in the sky
The larks, still bravely singing, fly
Scarce heard amid the guns below.

We are the dead. Short days ago
We lived, felt dawn, saw sunset glow,
Loved and were loved, and now we lie
In Flanders' fields.

Take up our quarrel with the foe;
To you from failing hands we throw
The torch; be yours to hold it high,
If ye break faith with us who die
We shall not sleep, though poppies grow
In Flanders' Fields.

On the eleventh hour of the eleventh day of the eleventh month in 1918 the First World War ended. People wanted to remember those who had given their lives for peace and freedom. An American War Secretary, Moina Michael, inspired by John McCrae's poem, began selling poppies to friends to raise money for the ex-Service community and so the tradition began.

In 1922, Major George Howson, a young infantry officer, formed the Disabled Society, to help disabled ex-Service men and women from the First World War. Howson suggested to the Legion that members of the Disabled Society could make poppies and the Poppy Factory was subsequently founded in Richmond in 1922. The original poppy was designed so that workers with a disability could easily assemble it and this principle remains today.

"and the leaves of the tree were for the healing of the nations"

The Croxley branch of the Legion used to hold their meetings in the Science Room of the Guild House, but about 1953 they were able to use the Territorial Headquarters just off the Green for social events. Major Peyton had been president for some years followed by Lt. Colonel Goad who was also President around 1958. The World War Two members wanted to build their headquarters on a site in Watford Road but Lt Colonel Goad and the First World War members were worried about carrying a heavy mortgage. Members got together and with the help of Jacko and Harold Picton, who owned a bulldozer, they cleared the site. The walls were built to ceiling height free of charge and members set to with a will. The building was opened in 1958. The Churchill Lounge was added in 1965 and opened the following year."

Keep Croxley 'Green' Group

The group was formed in 2004 by concerned residents in response to a planning application by London Underground Ltd/Metronet to build a rail track replacement depot on the Green Belt site known as Buddleia Walk just south of Long Valley Wood. The group's main project is to obtain the registration of the whole 30-acre site that forms both the Buddleia Walk and Long Valley Wood as a Village Green and to save it in perpetuity for local residents to enjoy their local sports and pastimes. At the time of writing LUL has withdrawn their application. To date the land has been recognised as a Wildlife Site and part of the wood qualify for the status of Ancient Woodland.

The Croxley Green Mummers - A Christmas Tradition

One of the many English Christmas customs is that of the Mummers play. These plays were a traditional form of village entertainment and can be found in slightly different forms in many areas of England. Croxley has its very own version of the play. All the plays tell the story of the hero, usually St George who is at first killed by the Dragon and revived by the Doctor. He then goes on to kill the Dragon, the Turkish Knight and the Giant and, finally, he wins the hand of the King of Egypt's daughter.

Croxley's version of the play was written by 'Neggy' Wilson and is a compilation of bits from other plays from around the country. Neggy, one of Croxley's well known characters, was the headmaster of the Croxley Boys School. He got together a group of his former pupils to perform the play in Croxley Green. It was performed nearly every year from the 1920s until the late 1950s. Some of the early actors were Stan Lyons, Fred Randall, Frank Paddick, and the three Samuels brothers; later members of the cast included Bert Sadler, Albert Seabrook, Don Webb and John and Michael Thomas.

In 1994 a group of Croxley residents decided that it might be an idea to try to revive the play and perform it at Christmas time. Actors were recruited and the members set about making costumes and rehearsing. Unfortunately the original Croxley costumes were destroyed in the fire at the Dickinson Guild House in 1965. The original revival cast members were George Paddick, Alan Monahan, Madryn Waldron, Margaret Pomfret, Nigel Moorcroft, Dave and Michele Bennett, John Quick and David Hillier. Some more recent members of the cast have included: Bob and Hilary Parnell, Roger Cattermoul, Tim Davis, and Graham Sawyer.

The group had problems with theatre licences but eventually this was sorted out and the play has been performed on the Sunday before Christmas ever since.

In days gone by the mummers usually started off at All Saints' Vicarage and, as most of the cast were workers at Dickinson's Mill, they finished at Lindiswara Court which was the home of Charles Barton-Smith, who was the manager of the Mill.

The Jazz Workshop is an informal co-operative venture run by musicians for musicians. Members meet at the Sportsman every Monday night at 8 p.m. It provides an opportunity for musicians new to playing jazz to try things out in an informal friendly atmosphere, with no 'schoolroom' feel, while more experienced players get together to try out new ideas and practice their ensemble playing.

Dave and I spent a happy time with some people who have allotments in Croxley Green.

Naturally, by the Pilgrim family, Richmond Way is considered to be the very heart of Croxley Green if not the universe because I was born there! Having (modestly) stated this fact, the street was certainly the centre of my world until I reached around twelve years old. I delivered milk and greengrocery to its inhabitants, collected the dung from the greengrocer's and baker's horses for my father's garden from the road and watched Denis Compton score the winning runs in a Test Match on the Garlick family's television (believed to be one of the first TV sets in our road).

My mum had nicknames for some of Richmond Way's residents: There was 'Fireman Smith' and 'The Minister Scott', for example. A mother and son lived in Richmond Way for many years and the son became a bit of a legend for us youngsters. 'Bill' dressed in American style clothes, smoked American cigarettes and chewed American gum! Every evening, or so it seemed, Bill would dress up and catch the 385 bus to Watford where he would have a few drinks in the aptly named 'Oddfellows Arms' before catching the last bus back to Croxley. As teenagers we would also board that last bus safe in the knowledge that Bill would be sitting on the back seat, upstairs, ready to offer us a piece of gum and a cigarette. Many years later my brothers and I were talking about those days and got to wondering what happened to Bill. I contacted my friend 'Ollie' Phillips at the Watford Observer and he was able to supply us with a rather sad report from the newspaper. It seems that a man walking his dog along the towpath of the canal came upon a pile of clothes neatly stacked on the path. He also saw a body floating in the canal. The report explained that Bill's mother had recently passed away and that Bill had been depressed since her passing. I thought that this was a particularly sad end for a man who had devoted his life to his mum and who was well respected in our road.

Richmond Way was also the practice area as far as cricket and football was concerned. Croxley was then, and indeed still is, particularly well served when it comes to open spaces but kids being kids will always play in the street! And so our cricket stumps were set up at the top of our driveway (adjoining Mr. Scott's house) and my run up began across the road from the Garlicks' house. Very few cars used Richmond Way and I don't ever recall having to halt my run to the wicket to deliver the tennis ball to a terrified John Fisher. The alleyway between numbers 14 and 12 was also Wimbledon Centre Court where I ceaselessly bounced a tennis ball against the wall of Mr. Scott's house. He never complained, even when we 'nicked' the twigs from the Golden Rod growing in his front garden to use as arrows to fire through the spokes of my dad's bike as he returned home for lunch from Mrs. Woodhouse's farm.

I explained earlier in this book how a certain Colonel Goad was responsible for my departure from Rickmansworth Grammar before the anticipated time. I decided to check out exactly who this gentleman was and it proved a lot more difficult than I had expected. For a start all I had was a name and a rank: 'Colonel C.E. Goad M.C.' It seemed easy enough to check out all the Colonel Goads, find one who had an M.C. and I would be home and dry. However there turned out to be two or three Colonel Goads, some with military honours some without and it was then a matter of finding out which Goad was the Croxley Goad. My thanks for tracking the gentleman down go to Editor and Researcher Margaret Ward and my brother Bill.

COUNTY ALDERMAN COLONEL C.E. GOAD M.C.

Cecil Elliot Godfrey Boileau Goad was born in 1885 in India where his father Joseph was a District Superintendent of Police, Bengal. Cecil was a career soldier and his first commission was in 1905 with the 128th Pioneers, Indian Army. He was made a Lieutenant in 1907 and we think that he remained with the Pioneers throughout the First World War. In August 1917 he was awarded the M.C. and by this time he was Captain Goad.

We know that he was in Croxley Green by 1920 because he married Mary Joyce Woolrych, who was the daughter of Lt Colonel Humphrey Woolrych of Croxley House. At the time of his marriage Cecil was a Major. In 1923 the Goads had a daughter and were living at Parrots on the Green. In 1937 Cecil became the local Civil Defence organiser and then through the Second World War he was County Sub Controller for the South West area of Hertfordshire. At some time the Goads moved from Parrotts to Clare Cottage on the Green. The Colonel left the area in 1959 because of ill health and he died in 1960 at Lee on Solent. I wonder if he and my headmaster had a bit of a laugh after they banished me from Ricky Grammar School. The headmaster might have but I doubt if a career soldier such as Goad would have found my poor disciplinary record very funny!

ICE CREAM SUNDAYS

It's true that the ice cream man paid a visit to our road on weekdays but somehow Sunday was special and we were spoilt for choice in Croxley because we had not one but two fabulous ice cream men to choose from. They were both Italian of course, only the best ice cream for Croxley and Watford residents. It is quite amazing the things you remember from your childhood, why would I be certain that the man who delivered ice cream for Mazzone's had spectacles? Even more interesting is the fact that the name Grillo, which will forever be associated with ice cream for me, is still a well known name in the area. First here is part of an article from the Watford Observer; K.J. Cooper, of Oxhey, wrote: "On summer Sundays round about 1930, old Mr. Grillo (probably Matteo) would arrive opposite the Duke of York pub which is located in Watford Road, Croxley Green, in his pony and trap. For three old pence he would fill a glass beaker with his delicious ice cream. He also sold it as half-penny and penny cornets and as tuppenny wafers of a half-inch of ice cream between biscuit wafers made in a hand held contraption. In the weeks before Christmas he would appear again, but this time it was with fruit and nuts. I particularly remember the boxes of 25 tangerines with each segment having at least one pip (forerunner of satsuma and mandarin oranges) with alternate ones wrapped in silver paper." K. J. Cooper's memories date from the 1930s, mine are from the 1940s and to cap it all there is an actor called John Grillo who was born in Watford in the same year as me! I am reliably informed that the very same Mr. John Grillo either lived or lives in Croxley Green. Ice cream has never been as good as it was back then. We waited for the sound of the ice cream man to enter our road and looked longingly at Mum and Dad to see if they were able and willing to cough up the cost of a cone or a wafer. There was only one other ice cream around to challenge Mazzone's or Grillo's and that was in Chiswick where my auntie Doris worked at Milos in the High Road but that had more than a little to do with getting a 'freebie'.

ANOTHER MYSTERY SOLVED

Earlier I explained how we used a piece of land in Croxley as our very own golf course and that there had been a large house on the land when I was a kid. All that is left now is a crumbling wall and some evidence of the orchard and other specimen trees. After David Thrower had taken some shots of the wall and the trees we walked along the towpath on the canal to take some shots of the lock keeper's cottage. It was then that I realised that the land behind the cottage would have been the 'back garden' of the house which overlooked Croxley Green and Rousebarn Lane. Further investigation revealed some work carried out by David Setford at Watford Museum. David found that the Ordnance Survey map of the area in 1910 showed a large house on the land where we used to play golf. The local Kelly's Directories revealed some of the names of the people in residence. Walter Seymour Greves lived there and further investigation indicated that there had been a house on the land in 1850. The house was purchased by Edwin Meekings and in 1924 by Major Osman B. Gabriel who lived at the house until 1940. It then became the headquarters of Associated British Film Distributors until the early sixties when it was demolished. Watford Museum claims Cassiobridge House is its own but for my money it is part of Croxley Green!

Did He or Didn't He?

I have always been led to believe that a certain Bedford Jezzard who played soccer for Fulham and England began his career in Croxley Green and I managed to find some evidence to support this claim. In the records for Durrants School held at Croxley library there is a signed photograph of Jezzard. This led me to make further enquiries and I came up with the following from a website about Fulham Football Club;

'Bedford Jezzard born Clerkenwell, London 1927 made his senior debut on the twenty third of May 1954, clubs Croxley Green School, Croxley Green Juniors, Watford FC (Amateur) and Fulham, made his international debut against Hungary and retired through injury 1957'. So there is some substance to the story but which Croxley team did Jezzard play for? I do know that he went on to manage Fulham FC and then ran a pub in London but that is all. The photograph below seems to indicate that the 'Croxley School' could have been Durrants.

Bedford Jezzard in what looks to me to be Fulham colours

Croxley had some other sporting heroes during the 1940s and Durrants School provided most of them.

For a while my brother George worked at Glikstens beside the canal, where they stored timber destined to be used as coffin boards. The timber was delivered by barges on the canal and a crane was used to move them onto the site. A regular lunch break pastime probably made my brother one of the first 'bungee jumpers' in the entire world. George would place his foot in the hook at the base of the crane and the driver would raise him into the air above the canal and then release the brake, thus George would hurtle towards the water! Health and Safety procedures being non-existent at the time, George and his mates would spend their lunch breaks blissfully unaware of the dangers involved in such pursuits.

Just a short distance from Glikstens there was a stainless steel gun emplacement left over from the Second World War. I guess that it was there to be used for a machine gun should the Germans arrive. I have also been informed that, because 'Jerry' used the canal to navigate their aircraft to London, there was some kind of a boat on the waterway which was fitted with a gun to attack the planes.

It all looks very different now but this was the area where coffin boards were stored and George 'bungee jumped'

CROXLEY PARK

Croxley Business Park stands on the edge of Common Moor and, at least for me, has a certain charm. There are many sparkling, brand new buildings standing in pleasant surroundings with plenty of water fountains and landscaped areas to ease the furrowed brows of the workers as they make their way to and from their daily toil. The problem with this area is the fact that all that exists of the Sun Engraving Company building is the clock tower. The company played an important part in the life of many residents of Croxley much in the same way as Dickinson's Mill did. When I was growing up the people who worked at 'The Sun' were the 'crème de la crème', they earned good money and could afford many of the luxuries that we lesser mortals could not. The Sun Engraving Company also contributed to the war effort, as we shall see.

THE SUN AT WAR

At the end of the First World War, a London based company called André Sleigh & Anglo Ltd. purchased the premises of Menpes Press in Watford and, in 1919 they took the name the Sun Engraving Company. In 1941 they were printing propaganda leaflets for the Government and the initial output consisted of over 200,000 units. Over the next four years the Sun printed booklets, small magazines, posters and a German language daily newspaper. The Sun also began secret experiments for ICI. These experiments and the Sun's production work on the gaseous diffusion process helped with the development of the atomic bomb. For the Air Ministry the company produced loose-leaf books of aerial reconnaissance photographs covering strategic bombing targets and tactical operations. The Sun finally closed in 2004 after having had spectacular success with such national magazines as *Woman's Own*.

Roundabout

Sun Clock

Keith Donald Warn was born in Croxley Green, on the 20th March 1941. He made three appearances for Watford Football Club in the football league and his football career included playing for London Schools, Croxley Boys Club, Fulham youth team; Watford, Dover, Kettering Town, Stevenage Town, Elizabeth City, Australia, Modbury, Australia and Sun Sports (by 1972/73). He was Dickinsons (Croxley) social manager (until 1977).

After his success as a goalkeeper at Durrants School he went on to play for the county youth team. His three league appearances were in a Watford team on the verge of winning promotion from the Fourth Division, and he began with two clean sheets. He also played occasionally in the forward line, for both the youth team and the reserves. His mum allowed me to leave my bike in her front garden on the days I went to school! I also worked for Keith's dad Bert on occasions, he was a local builder.

The following is a report of a game at Vicarage Road in April 1960 when two Croxley lads showed off their skills in a Football League Division 4 game: "Keith Warn deputising for Jimmy Linton in goal seemed to be rather short for a goalie, but made some spectacular saves that day (I guess Gateshead must have got the ball a few times, after all) and Mike Benning a vertically challenged player appeared to be attached to the greyhound wire on the right wing. This is the only plausible explanation for the pinpoint crosses he delivered all afternoon". The result was Watford Five – Gateshead Nil.

Mike or Mick Benning as he was known to his mates lived in Warwick Way, Croxley and had a somewhat nostalgic affect on my mum! Mick took the Benning family dog for a walk last thing at night and he would amble past our house whistling contentedly. For the five years that brother George was away in Australia Mick's whistling would remind Mum of her 'Wild Colonial Boy' who had left home at the age of seventeen, carrying a small holdall to discover the world. George was also an inveterate whistler and Mick's nightly twittering brought back memories for her.

Peter Biegel was born in Croxley Green on 22nd April 1913, into an artistic family. One of his ancestors was Frederick Sang, a well known artist and architect. His family were renowned horsemen and his great-grandfather was killed in a steeplechase at the age of twenty-one. Peter's father was Dutch and, because of his prowess as a horseman, naturally enough known as the 'Flying Dutchman' in the hunting field. Biegel took naturally to art from a very early age. He was educated at Downside School, which I believe is near Bath, and then went into his father's business in the city. After five years he decided to study art seriously and in 1938 became a student at Lucy Kemp-Welch's school at Bushey. When World War Two broke out he obtained a TA commission in the Wiltshire Regiment. He was invalided back from Normandy in 1944, and was posted to Northern Ireland as a claims officer. Biegel painted horse portraits, both racing and hunting, and also action pictures of both subjects. A number of his works have been reproduced as prints and also on cigarette cards but for me, his greatest achievement has to be the fact that he illustrated one of Enid Blyton's books. *Six Cousins At Mistletoe Farm* is quite rare so if you come across a copy let me know. The Kelly's Directory of 1914 lists a Carl Biegel as residing at the Nook in Croxley, I assume that this was Peter's birthplace. Peter Biegel died in 1988.

Anyone who has ever been invited to "blow into this" by a doctor, or by a traffic policeman will probably have encountered an instrument developed by Martin Wright. These were characteristically simple, compact pieces of precision engineering that have become design classics in the medical world. Asthmatics, the terminally ill, and premature babies are the primary beneficiaries of his medical inventions; but he also made an important contribution to road safety in developing the most commonly used roadside breathalyzer. He was born in 1912, the second son of a clergyman, and educated at Winchester and Trinity College, Cambridge. He graduated from Cambridge with a first class degree in Physiology, did his clinical training at St Bartholomew's Hospital, and graduated in medicine in 1938. In 1942 he enlisted in the Royal Army Medical Corps as a pathologist, to research the physiological effects of tank warfare. He rose to the rank of colonel by the end of the Second World War, while reconstructing medical laboratory services in Singapore. These experiences, requiring maximum improvisation with minimum equipment, gave him his first opportunity to develop his natural flair for engineering.

We found a record of a Dr. B. M. Wright living at Scots Hill House in 1973 and, although he seemed to move around the area quite a bit, I am pretty sure that this was home to the family for a while. We found an obituary which states that he died at Croxley Green.

Terry Scott's mum lived in Croxley Green, on Kenilworth Drive. If you have no idea who Terry Scott was, you are too young to be reading this book! Terry was born in Watford in 1927. He was the son of a retired postman, who ran a corner shop. He trained as an accountant and served in the Royal Navy during the Second World War, before embarking on an acting career. He appeared in many *Carry On films* and had his first real success on television with Bill Maynard in a comedy series entitled *Great Scott It's Maynard*. He went on to appear in a massive hit series called *Terry and June* with that fine actress June Whitfield. In later life he was considered to be one of the finest pantomime dames of his generation. Terry died in 1994.

This is a really tenuous link because it relies on memory alone. In the 1960s there was a hit television game show called *Take Your Pick*. It starred a man called Michael Miles and included a really interesting man named Bob Danvers Walker. He is interesting because it was his voice that was heard on the Pathe Newsreels in the cinemas. You will recall (if you have been reading every page of this book and not skipping bits) that Pathe had an operation which distributed film via Croxley. The aforementioned *Take Your Pick* programme included a 'Yes / No Interlude' where contestants could win cash by not answering yes or no to any of the questions posed by Michael Miles. If you could last a full sixty seconds you won the cash! If you couldn't, a man called Alec Dane would bang a gong to signify your defeat. And the point is that my mum insisted that Alec Dane, an actor and singer, lived in a house on Croxley Green, if that isn't fame I don't know what is. Stop Press! I met a man who can confirm that Bob Danvers Walker did live in Croxley Green. Mr. Milson Watkins, who has lived in Croxley for many years confirmed that the aforementioned Danvers Walker had a house on The Green at one time.

London cabbie Fred Housego was living in Croxley Green when he took part in the TV show *Mastermind*, the show was hosted by Magnus Magnussen and created by TV producer, Bill Wright who had been an RAF gunner in World War Two. Wright based part of the show on the three things he had been taught to give if he ever became a prisoner of war (and he did): 'Name, Rank and Number'. Contestants were asked name, occupation and specialist subject.

Whenever anyone speaks about *Mastermind* they always come up with the name Fred Housego, but in fact he was not the first taxi driver to appear on the show, Robert Smith holds that distinction, but it was Housego who grabbed the nation's attention. The 1980 champion came from St John's Wood in London and left school at the age of sixteen with one 'O' level. He took 'Henry II of England' on the first programme he appeared in and he won. He actually watched his second appearance from an Intensive Care Unit where he had been taken with a suspected heart attack. Housego recovered and won the semi-final with 'The Collegiate Church of St Peter at Westminster' as his subject. For the final Fred picked 'The Tower of London' and scored eighteen points and fifteen on general knowledge to set a target of thirty three for his rival, but would our hero win the title? His closest rival Samuel Mortimer achieved thirty one points and Fred Housego captured the imagination of the nation as Magnus Magnusson spoke these words: 'There will be rejoicing in the ranks tonight!' A comment worthy of myself, I think Magnus. I had breakfast with Fred Housego once and as I recall, I paid.

The 1901 census shows a Seymour W. Greves living on Scots Hill. Mr. Greves founded the Burlington Glove and Fan Depot at Burlington Arcade, London and he had a shop in Oxford Street which he lived above before moving to Croxley Green.

Also appearing in the 1901 census we find Frederick Frayer, a diamond merchant from Cricklewood who had moved to a property between Scots Hill and Yorke Road. Anyone know 'Hollow Tree House'?

Scots Hill House in 1901 was home to one Charles Kennedy, a 'Partner in a brewery'.

THE WAR MEMORIAL

The memorial stands on Croxley Green just opposite New Road. It is of particular interest not simply for its design but for the fact that someone saw fit to include the Korean War. I once travelled on H.M.S. Belfast when she was travelling down the Thames on her way to Portsmouth for a refit. On the journey I was privileged to speak with several men who had served in Korea, as indeed did the Belfast. These men felt that the war in Korea was a forgotten war and so it is good to know that the people of Croxley Green have done their bit to put the matter right. All war memorials are moving but for me the one at Croxley is special because there are so many names that I remember from my childhood. When I was growing up I knew nothing of the hardship endured not only by the brave people who fought for our country but by their loved ones who also served in so many different ways. One cannot stand in front of such a memorial without feeling both pride and humility.

The War Memorial

Built as 'temporary' accommodation at the end of the Second World War, these homes are often recalled with great affection by those who lived in them and I can understand why. The prefabs came to Croxley in 1946 when the country was struggling to find homes for servicemen and women who were returning to 'civvy street'.

The prefabs in Croxley were in Grove Crescent and many of my school friends lived there. Michael McKinley, who now lives 'up north', moved in with his family in 1947. He describes the development as quite remarkable and, although his family moved out after just two years, he continued to visit and to play with the friends he had made. I met Mike a few years ago at a school reunion and he told me that he intended to write a history of life in a prefab. I look forward to reading it.

The gardens were always well kept and well used to supply household food and veg

In 1944 the Americans stationed at nearby Bovingdon, having seen vehicles struggling up Scots Hill, make an offer to the council. If the hill is closed for a week the Yanks will bring in one thousand men to work on the hill, flatten it, regrade it and tarmac the surface.

In 1940 a local man was caught cycling home with two bags of black market sugar in his basket. He was charged but then suffered the indignity of having to listen to the locals whistling 'Ain't She Sweet' whenever he went out on his bike!

The German Air Force dropped their bombs on Cassiobury Park in 1940 and local youths collected some memorabilia. They also stood on West Herts golf course to watch a Spitfire attempting to shoot down a barrage balloon that was drifting between the fourth and fifth holes.

In 1911 a bandstand and public conveniences were promised for Cassiobury Park.

In 1926 Mussolini survived an attempt on his life after a bullet clipped his nose. This didn't happen in Croxley but I thought it might interest someone because not a lot of people nose that!

In 1947 (I was five years old) the area experienced its coldest winter for fifty years and the worst flooding of the river Colne for twenty years.

In 1959 Barbara Woodhouse's dog appeared as the hound in the Hammer Film production of *The Hound of the Baskervilles*.

In the 1930s Daphne Du Maurier paid several visits to her father Sir Gerald who lived at Rackets and wrote:

Croxley days, the birds singing, and Mo wandering about gardening, the children in sun bonnets. It was good to be in the country after the dust and noise of London and he wandered about with a book on birds in one hand and a book on wild flowers in the other, dressed in shabby tweeds, with a spy-glass round his neck, and Angela and Daphne trotting at his heel.

On the 22nd of April 1905 the *Herts Advertiser* reported that two ladies from Watford were summoned for obstructing the pavement with perambulators! The two mothers were fined 2s 6d each and costs of 3s 9d. The Chairman of the bench described the manner in which the women obstructed the pavement as "an intolerable nuisance". A letter in a copy of the *Hertfordshire Countryside* magazine appears to confirm this attitude. It seems that when Cassiobury Park was first opened to the public, parents had to have a permit for their prams.

In 1954 I fell in love seriously for the very first time after seeing Doris Day in the movie *Calamity Jane*. The sad thing is that so did Dudley Withers, Peter Priggen and Alan Smith. We even named the trolley that we built ,'Calam'.

In 1958 I fell in love with a Swedish girl who was visiting Peter Priggen's family and she showed more than a passing interest in me, which was good considering that she was two years older than I was. She only stayed for two weeks and when she left she took my St Christopher with her. On reflection it served her right that it was a cheap imitation and not silver as I had told her.

In 1924 when Rickmansworth Road was going to be paved residents complained, saying that it would not be good for the "preservation of the rural character of the road".

In 1927 squirrels had become such pests in Cassiobury Park that the authorities gave the Park Keeper a gun to shoot on sight.

The LMS tip near Croxley Station caught fire and managed to keep burning through a massive storm, it is said that the fire burned through the year of 1925. The following year the first council houses appeared in Croxley on Springwell Avenue.

Would you believe that in 1938 people were picnicking on West Herts Golf Course and disrupting play!

It was announced that six hundred and fifty six houses would be built on part of the Durrants Estate in 1934 – in the same year the council opposed plans for a road through Whippendell Woods. Sometimes councils get things right, then.

In 1949 I fell over in the snow on the way to school (across the spare land where Norwich Way is now). I am pleased to report that I still have the scar and that I managed to wangle a whole week off school.

In 2006, I am reliably informed that some of the scenes for the Harry Potter movies were shot in Croxley Green.

I picked up the following item of interest from the *Watford Observer*.

A Pest House used to be situated near the river Chess at Croxley and a resident of the village, a Mr. David Neighbour, sent the following information to the newspaper: Pest houses were also known as plague houses and were used as isolation homes for people who had come into contact with contagious diseases such as smallpox. The homes were funded locally, by the church and local benefactors. The Croxley pest house stood near the Chess where the names Pest House Field and Pest House Meadow still bear reference to it. The house was probably in use from the 17th century through to the mid 19th century and Mr. Neighbour recalls the ruins of an old red brick building with a triple Tudor chimney which was eventually pulled down in the 1950s.

It must have been in the 1960s when one of my brother George's drinking pals played a few games for Watford FC. His name was 'Dodger' Beaumont. There is a story that tells how 'Dodger', who was a goalkeeper and rather well built, dived in front of an on rushing centre forward and was kicked on the head. The centre forward broke his ankle.

Shirley Greenman lives in Croxley Green and she wrote a most interesting book entitled *A History of Croxley Green Through Its Street Names*. I thoroughly recommend the book to you.

In May 1945 the *Watford Observer* reported that Mr. and Mrs. L. Jacobs of Highfield, Scots Hill owned a piano that Franz Liszt played on a visit to England in 1886 and that it had been loaned to All Saints for a recital.

In 1949 there was a fireproof floor company registered in Croxley Hall Woods.

In the same year a certain J. Beeson M.S.F. certified masseur (joint manipulation) lived at number 48 Dickinson Avenue.

The following pages contain some photographs which might stir a few memories.

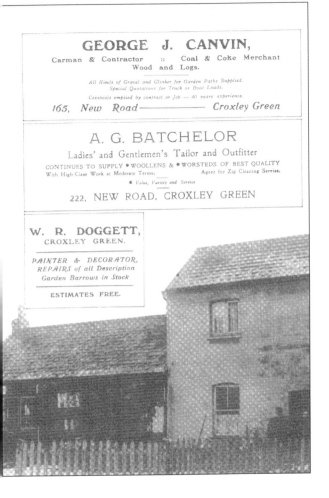

BIBLIOGRAPHY

A History of Croxley Green Through its Street Names – Shirley Greenman, Croxley Parish Council ISBN 09528036 07

The History of Croxley House – Mildred Green, Greensleeves Homes Trust.

A History of Redheath and York House School – Patrick B. Moore

An Outline History of Croxley – Croxley Green Local History Group 1950, Hertfordshire Archives & Local Studies; www.croxleygreen.com

Croxley Revels website

Mike Stanyon, Dickinson Paper Trail

Herts Countryside Management, Hertfordshire County Council.

Watford Observer

Herts Advertiser

This book is dedicated to my Mum and Dad, Ivy Dorothy Pilgrim and Arthur George Pilgrim and to my brothers and sisters, June Rose O'Mahoney, Bill Pilgrim, George Pilgrim, Linda Seeley and Susan Scott and to their long suffering partners and spouses who, throughout the years have suffered the vagaries of being associated with a somewhat eccentric family! I would not have survived this world without their support. God bless them.

Also by John Pilgrim

Out and About with John Pilgrim
Photography by David Spain

Out and About Again with John Pilgrim
Photography by David Spain

The Very Best Out and About Book
Photography by David Spain

The Barnsdale Handy Gardener
Photography by David Thrower

All Published by Alpine Press Ltd.

Copies of 'Out & About in Croxley Green' can be obtained directly from Alpine Press.

Email: sales@alpine-press.co.uk

Please enclose a cheque for £9.95 plus £1.30 for postage and packaging for each copy.

David Thrower established Redshift Photography in 2003, having worked in the photographic field for many years. His passion for the subject from an early age, coupled with extensive and varied experience, has evolved into the distinct and original style which is evident in his work today. Beginning in sports photography, he then moved into the lighting industry as a lighting designer which enabled him to develop an in-depth understanding of artificial light sources and how light and form combine to create stunning visual impact.

Copies of the photographs in this book which were taken by David can be purchased direct from Redshift Photography mounted and signed.

Email: david.thrower@redshift-photography.co.uk

David Thrower - ARPS Photographer and MD &
Melanie Thrower - Commercial Director

John Pilgrim can be contacted at john.pilgrim1@virgin.net

THE NORTH END BOYS

According to an item in the Watford Observer dated 14th October 1916 the 'North End Boys' were a Croxley football team before World War I, the majority being members of the Croxley Lads Brigade. Most of the team were killed in the Great War. The Observer states: "Of the 35 Croxley Lads Brigade who rushed to the colours at the outbreak of war, only six or seven remain in the fighting line, the others being killed or wounded." Roger Bennett has put together a delightful collection of songs in his 'A Croxley Song Book' (on view at Croxley Library) and I thought that it would be appropriate to include one here about the 'North End Boys' written in the early 1900s.

'It Was Last Christmas Morning'

It was last Christmas morning as on the Green we stood,
When one of us proposed a stroll to Chorleywood,
We started from the Artichoke with hearts so full and free
But to learn the story proper, just listen now to me.

There was also Foreman Owen
And Grady, big and bold,
But to cut our story shorter
We were twenty four all told.

Then up the Green we strolled
Along Loudwater Lane,
The twenty four all told
To Chorleywood all came.

We gazed at one another,
Then hanging out his tongue,
Jock Adams that old blighter
Said, thy will be done.

We called in at the White Horse
It's Mrs Sales you know,
And for to shift her beer
Not one of us was slow.

Some of us had bottled ale,
Some others they had gin
Then after blowing out our hides
We all sat down to sing.